TRANSFORMING
FRIENDSHIP

Contents

Acknowledgements

This book has been a long time in the making and I am extremely grateful to so many of my friends who have patiently listened to my ramblings and have provided insights, comments, criticisms and feedbacks. In particular I want to thank the following (in alphabetical order) with apologies to anyone that I have inadvertently left out: Christopher Ash, Steve Beck, Jenny Brown, Ben Chang, Ellidh Cook, Andrew Cornes, Mary Currie, Timothy Dudley-Smith, Janet Goodall, John Greenall, Glynn Harrison, Mark Hunt, Edwin Hutson, Mercy Abraham Imondi, Mark Labberton, Dick Lucas, Roy McCloughry, Mark Meynell, Martin Mills, David Zac Niringiye, Ruth Padilla DeBorst, Hugh Palmer, Richard Parrish, Daniel Porter, Sunil Raheja, Vinoth Ramachandra, Steve Richardson, Matthew Smith, Steve Sturman, Rico Tice, Andrzej Turkanik, David Turner, Ed Veale, Paula V, Rob Wilson, Chris Wright, Andrew Wyatt, Beka Wyatt, Celia Wyatt, Emma Wyatt, Jess Wyatt, Jonathan Wyatt and Tim Wyatt.

Thank you to my many friends, named and unnamed. Writing this book has made me much more aware of how precious your friendship has been in my life, and of my many shortcomings and failings as a friend in return. May this book be a small tribute and token of gratitude for the richness and joy you have brought into my life, and what you have shown me about the heart of the Father.

A special thanks to my wife Celia who has patiently encouraged and supported me through long periods of despair and doubt about this project.

I am particularly grateful to the two IVP editors who have helped me navigate the challenges of bringing this book to birth: Eleanor Trotter, who encouraged and advised me in the early stages, and Josh Wells, for his encouragement, patience and perseverance. Special thanks also to Mary Davis for wise advice and meticulous editing of the final manuscript. I am of course responsible for any errors or inaccuracies that remain.

Text acknowledgements

Unless otherwise stated, scripture quotations are from the ESV Bible (The Holy Bible, English Standard Version), copyright © 2001 by Crossway, a publishing ministry of Good News Publishers. Used by permission. All rights reserved.

Scripture quotations marked NIV are taken from The New International Version (Anglicized edition). Copyright © 1979, 1984, 2011 by Biblica. Used by permission of Hodder & Stoughton Ltd, an Hachette UK company. All rights reserved. 'NIV' is a registered trademark of Biblica. UK trademark number 1448790.

Scripture quotations marked KJV are taken from The Authorized (King James) Version. Rights in the Authorized Version in the United Kingdom are vested in the Crown. Reproduced by permission of the Crown's patentee, Cambridge University Press.

Quotations on pp. 44–45, 62 and 156 taken from *The Four Loves* by C. S. Lewis copyright © C. S. Lewis Pte. Ltd, 1960; p. 82 from 'The Inner Ring' in *The Weight of Glory* by C. S. Lewis copyright © C. S. Lewis Pte. Ltd, 1944, 1949; p. 157 from *Letters to Malcolm* by C. S. Lewis copyright © C. S. Lewis Pte. Ltd, 1963, 1964. Extracts reprinted by permission.

Introduction

I turn from the bustling central London street into the quiet cobbled mews, as I had many times before. Memories flood back. As I walk towards the entrance of the tiny flat, I glance up to the window to see if the desk is occupied. Approaching the door I experience a mixture of anticipation and slight trepidation. I touch the buzzer and the familiar, instantly recognisable voice is on the speaker. 'Come up, my dear brother.' I climb the narrow circular staircase and enter the book-lined study.

It is the late 1970s. I am a recently qualified doctor, working as an intern in a central London hospital. And the person I have come to see is John Stott. He is at the peak of his international Christian ministry, a revered Bible teacher, writer and preacher – already being recognised as one of the most influential Christian leaders of the twentieth century. As I approached that door, I was finding it hard to believe that John Stott should choose to spend hours of his precious time alone with me. And more than forty years later I still find it strange and wonderful. An unlooked-for gift of God's grace.

At the time I had no idea of what lay ahead, the various projects that we would engage in, the lessons I would learn, the trips we would take together. Years later, I suffered a major psychiatric illness and was admitted to a locked hospital ward. He tracked me down and telephoned me in the hospital. I can still remember his compassionate words in the midst of my internal agony, depression and confusion. 'I value your friendship, John.' His love and sensitivity brought tears to my eyes then, and I still weep in thankfulness now as I remember that time.

Years later again, he suffered a serious accident, fracturing a hip and requiring major surgery. I had the privilege of spending hours with him – both in the hospital as he slowly recovered and when he returned to his bachelor flat. But the recognition that he would never again be able to live independently represented a deep loss and I remember one incident in particular, holding him in my arms as he wept uncontrollably.

We walked together, sharing our lives and hearts through triumphs, tragedies and health crises, from the 1970s until his death in 2011. And his friendship, vision and gentle godly influence were to become a defining factor in my life, changing the direction of my career, my preoccupations, my priorities and my ministry.

As time went by, I gradually became aware that there were in fact many young people like me whom Stott had quietly befriended. Some were students, interns and young professionals in London and the UK. Many were around the world – individuals whom he had met on his frequent international speaking trips and to whom he privately offered his friendship, sharing his wisdom, encouragement and prayers.

This was a hidden ministry, a private counterpoint to the public persona. It's an aspect of his life which seems to me to have received insufficient attention in the many biographies and retrospective assessments of his life and ministry. As far as I am aware, he rarely spoke in public or wrote in detail about his international ministry of friendship. Perhaps he would have regarded this as entirely inappropriate, unwise and a breach of confidentiality.

But judging from the time and energy that he devoted to friendships with people of all ages and backgrounds, male and female, there is little doubt that Stott saw this private and hidden ministry as one of the highest priorities of his life. He often went to extraordinary lengths to reach out to his friends around the world, spending countless hours in conversation and private correspondence. Many of us were invited on birdwatching trips, meals, reading groups and visits to concerts and plays. Each was an opportunity for deepening the relationship, for sharing his heart, for listening and encouraging. We received many handwritten letters in his tiny spidery writing, 'I haven't heard from you for some time. How are you? How can I pray for you? Do come and see me when you are next in London.'

How many people were being individually reached out to, prayed for, even pursued for the kingdom? I have no idea, but it must have run into hundreds if not thousands. And I suspect that, for all the impact and global reach of his public ministry, the lasting and profound impact of his personal friendship on hundreds of lives continues to this day and will continue across the generations long into the future.

This book is about gospel-shaped friendship, as we saw it modelled by John Stott, and as it has been practised over the centuries by countless followers of Christ. I have written out of my own personal experience and observation, and from conversations with others that Stott befriended and who have shared their own private experiences with me. Although he never spoke in detail about his personal practice of friendship to me, or as far as I am aware to many others, I have tried to piece together what can be discerned about his practices and patterns.

I have no doubt that friendship with John Stott transformed my own life. And I have become increasingly convinced that we need to put a far higher priority on friendship in our everyday Christian lives. Growing, nurturing and preserving deep, intimate, committed and loving friendships has always been an essential part of what it means to be a follower of Christ. It is not only my friendship with John Stott that has transformed my own life. I have been deeply blessed and privileged to have developed many close friends, both male and female, over my life. This book is dedicated to you, my dear friends. You know who you are, and I want to apologise to you right from the start for my many failings as a loyal and loving friend. I am afraid that I am better at the theory of friendship than actually putting it into practice! Some of my dearest friendships started in student days and they are still significant and life-enhancing for me fifty years later. Yet here in the early years of the twenty-first century, deep friendship between Christians seems to have become both strangely problematic and under-valued.

So in this book I will try to sustain an argument about friendship, about why it is so central to Christian discipleship, how it reflects the very character and heart of God himself, and how God uses friendship to love us and reveal his own heart, how it brings unique joy and comfort into our lives and is a precious foretaste of the life that is to come. Of course it is also essential to recognise that friendships can go wrong, that they can sometimes provide a context for terrible abuse and permanent damage. I will try to point out some dangers and red flags and suggest how, despite the risks, we can build and protect strong and intimate friendships which are crafted out of the heart of the gospel.

Although some of the book focuses on the particular opportunities and risks of intergenerational friendships, I hope that there is also enough here to inspire and encourage you in developing and deepening friendships with those of your own age. Perhaps you feel that, although you have some acquaintances, you don't have any real friends. Then I hope this book will encourage you and provide some realistic and practical pointers on how to build and nurture healthy friendships that reflect the characteristics of the gospel. I recognise that my perspective on friendship is that of a male, middle-class Brit of the baby-boomer generation. I have tried to include the voices and perspectives of people of different ages, cultures and gender, but human relationships are infinitely complex and fascinating and I am painfully aware of the limitations imposed by my own background and cultural blind spots.

We live in a very different world from that of the 1970s, when I first met John Stott. As I look back from the vantage of the 2020s, that previous world seems strikingly naive, trusting and unheeding. In the last few years the evangelical church has been rocked by revelations of spiritual and sexual abuse. It's a tragic litany of exploitation, misuse of power, coercion and manipulation of vulnerable individuals, predatory behaviour and mind-boggling hypocrisy. In the light of what we now know, John Stott's private activities could so easily be reinterpreted as manipulative, nepotistic, elitist, predatory, power-seeking, non-transparent and abusive. At the very least, trying to follow his example in developing such intimate intergenerational relationships might seem desperately unwise and inappropriate for the twenty-first century.

Inevitably I have gone back in my mind and reviewed everything I can remember of my friendship with him. Was there some unhealthy ulterior motive? Is it possible that I – and others – were being secretly coerced and manipulated? Were we being taken advantage of by a charming and sophisticated man of immense stature, intellect and reputation?

During my research for this book, I have had the privilege of talking to many of John Stott's close friends around the world. I have asked them the same questions. What was their experience of friendship with Stott and what did they learn? To those who wonder whether these pages will lead to shocking and disturbing revelations, I will either reassure or disappoint you. I have not come across any distressing or unexpected findings. I can honestly state that I have not become aware of any instance when any of Stott's closest friends felt manipulated, bullied, abused or coerced.

Of course, he was not perfect. He could be impatient with those who were stubborn or complaining. He found it hard to empathise with some who struggled with weakness or depression. He could at times, when he was tired and preoccupied, seem slightly distant and aloof. But he always treated us with an old-fashioned courtly respect. Although there were times of appropriate intimacy and self-revelation, there was also a sense of boundaries. If we overstepped the mark, we would be pushed back and gently put in our place.

But here in the 2020s we cannot ignore the current context of deep suspicion about intimate friendships, especially when there are obvious disparities of power and vulnerability. How is it that the modern world has come to perceive so many intimate friendships as driven ultimately by hidden self-centred psychological drives, especially the drive for sexual gratification or the desire to dominate and coerce?

In the first two chapters we explore these themes. Why should some close and emotionally open friendships be viewed as innately suspect and even 'creepy'? How did sex and power come to be seen as the dominant covert forces which motivate all deep and intimate relationships? Why have we become so suspicious? And what have we learnt about the immense potential for psychological, spiritual and emotional harm that abusive friendships can bring?

These are the painful realities, the complex and challenging landscape that provides the backdrop to any discussion of friendship in the twenty-first century, and we cannot avoid or escape the questions that they raise. There is no way back to the apparent naivety of previous generations and I have tried to address some of these challenging questions in what follows.

Having reviewed the evolution of ideas about friendship in the secular world we turn to the biblical perspective. We look at the biblical understanding of friendship, in both Old and New Testaments. It seems to have been a relatively neglected and under-explored theme for theologians and preachers over the last century, and yet there are deep riches to explore in the biblical narrative. How does the gospel of Jesus Christ challenge, subvert and redeem our understanding of the meaning and purpose of the deep bonds that can develop between broken human beings?

As David Zac Niringiye put it to me, the experience of a deep bond with John Stott was of a friendship which was 'carved out of the heart of the gospel'. It's an illuminating phrase and I have adopted the concept of gospel-shaped or gospel-crafted friendships as a model to reflect in more depth about John Stott, the fundamental characteristics of his relationships and what we can learn about the nature of healthy and transformative friendships.

In the next chapters I tell the story of my friendship with John Stott over more than thirty years, and how it transformed my own life, and then the personal stories of a small selection of John Stott's many friends around the world.

We then focus on the New Testament record of Paul's relationship with Timothy. Why is this relationship described in considerable detail in the pages of the New Testament and what can we learn from it that is relevant to today? What does this tell us about intergenerational gospel friendships, for both men and women, and how they differ from other forms of intentional one-to-one relationships that are now in vogue in parts of the Christian church – mentoring, coaching, pastoral care and so on?

In the following chapter we look at why and how friendship can go wrong. What are the ways in which sexual and coercive forces can corrupt and twist friendships, and what are the red flags that indicate that things are going wrong?

Next, we take a detour into the eighteenth and early nineteenth century and look at the central role of friendship in the lives of evangelical Christians in Britain at the time, including Charles Simeon whom Stott described as a formative historical role model for his own ministry. What role did close and intimate adult friendships play in the evangelical awakening and the transformative influence of the Clapham Sect?

In the final chapter, we will focus on practical issues. How can we reimagine Christian friendship in a form which is suitable for the twenty-first century? What can we do as a Christian community to encourage and foster healthy friendships – creating safe spaces in which our hearts and lives can be shared, nurtured and transformed by the life-giving gospel of Christ?

But first we turn to look at a brief history of friendship and why our default response has become so mistrustful and suspicious.

1

A brief history of friendship

As soon as we start to think about this topic, we run into a deep problem with the English language itself. The words 'friend' and 'friendship' have become so overused, distorted and trivialised in the twenty-first century that they have become virtually meaningless. A 'friend' can be mean everything and nothing. From one of thousands of trivial contacts on Facebook, to a passing acquaintance, to a work companion, to a sexual partner (a 'girlfriend' or 'boyfriend') to a lifelong intimate confidant. All can be described as 'friends'. Of course, all of us recognise a spectrum in our relationships: ranging from the relatively superficial contacts which probably number in the hundreds, through to perhaps twenty or more closer friends, through to, at most, a handful of people with whom we have a deep, intimate and self-disclosing relationship.

My interest and preoccupation in this book is with the small number of intimate and frequently lifelong bonds that change and transform our lives – for good or ill. I am a Christian believer and in my experience most, but not all, of my closest friendships are with those who share my Christian faith. So deep and committed friendships between Christians will be the main theme of this book. The word 'friend' for these relationships seems weak and trivial to modern ears. That Jesus should teach that there was no greater love than to lay down your life for *your friend*, seems strange. For your *child*, yes – for your *lover*, yes – but for your *friend*? Why on earth put friendship above these other far more significant bonds? Friendship seems just too weak, too insignificant to bear the full weight of self-sacrifice.

Think too of the passionate words penned by Samuel Crossman in 1664 in his hymn, 'My Song Is Love Unknown'.[1] In the last verse, at the final emotional climax of the piece, come the words, 'This is my friend, my friend indeed'. I suspect that many modern people as they sing those familiar phrases have found the choice of wording strange. Why not 'my Lord', 'my Saviour', 'my Bridegroom'?

On the other hand, when a relationship between two people starts to become particularly intimate, strong and close, especially when that friendship is between two men, the default instinct is to become suspicious. There must be something more than friendship, another deeper and more troubling motivation. Some kind of covert sexual attraction, an unhealthy emotional co-dependence, or an element of coercive manipulation? Things cannot just be what they seem.

This deep mistrust of intimate friendship is an example of what has been termed the 'hermeneutic of suspicion'. It's a corrosive and highly significant idea in our current culture and we will return to it later. But I am painfully aware that as soon as I start to describe the deep and intimate friendships which John Stott had with different people around the world, the hermeneutic of suspicion will be operating at red alert. What many of us suspect, and what the modern zeitgeist teaches us, is that behind all intimate, strong and committed relationships there are deep covert forces, most likely either sex or power and, in many cases, a toxic combination of both of these. There is no such thing as 'innocent', healthy friendships and those who maintain this fantasy are simply naive.

Take for example the descriptions of the intimate relationship between Jesus and 'the beloved disciple' in the fourth Gospel. The phrase 'the disciple whom Jesus loved' appears five times in the Gospel and in the literal Greek of John 13:23, he is described as 'reclining in the bosom of Jesus'. Astonishingly, it is exactly the same phrase which John has previously used to describe the intimacy of the relationship between God the Son and God the Father. 'The only begotten God who is *in the bosom* of the Father, he has made him known' (John 1:18). When we read of John reclining in Jesus' bosom with twenty-first-century eyes, the hermeneutic of suspicion seems overwhelming. Was this a homoerotic friendship between two single men which could only be revealed in the secrecy of the upper room? Was there a frisson of sexual chemistry involved? Or was this power play? Was the dominant and charismatic Jesus subtly manipulating the younger disciple through force of personality?

In a later chapter, we will return to the critical theme of how friendship is portrayed in the Gospels and in the Bible as a whole. But for now, I want to take on a very brief historical overview of how friendship has been viewed in previous ages. In this book I am consciously focusing on the positive aspects of friendship and how utterly transformative, joyful and liberating a healthy friendship can be. And yet at the same time I want to reflect on the dark side of friendship, on how close friendships can become corrupted by unhealthy and damaging forces, and how the corrosive atmosphere of suspicion has come to contaminate our perspectives on all friendships in the twenty-first century.

A statement attributed to the English archbishop William Temple is, 'If you don't know where you are going it is sometimes helpful to understand where you have been!'[2] So I make no apology for taking a historical approach in trying to understand how friendship in the modern world has become so contaminated, complex and even toxic.

Friendship in the classical world

It is important to start the story by looking at friendship in the world of classical Greece and Rome, partly because their ideas have been so influential in later Western civilisation, but also in order to emphasise how different classical models of friendship were from the Hebraic and biblical understanding. Friendship in the classical world was discussed and celebrated by many authors, but it is noticeable that the only friendship deemed worth writing about was that between people in elite social groups, and almost always that between men.[3] The classical authors distinguished between different forms of attraction. On the one hand there was *eros*, frequently referring to physical sexual attraction. This was often regarded as a powerful but irrational force which could even lead to a kind of madness. But the word when used by Plato could also be associated with a longing for the good and for the divine.

Another Greek word was *storge* which was mainly used for natural family affection, especially that between a parent and a child. And then there was *philia*, which was usually used for love between humans who were not related within a family. For Greek writers, *philia* was principally used for love orientated towards practical beneficence, doing good to the other. Aristotle praises *philia* as excellence in character, arguing that it was one of the virtues that should be celebrated and sought by all humans of good will. He divided *philia* into three categories depending on the goals of the relationship – friendship for good, friendship for pleasure and friendship which is useful. Of these, mutual friendship between virtuous equals based on goodness was considered the highest form, described as perfect friendship. 'Perfect friendship is the friendship of men who are good, and alike in excellence.'[4]

On the other hand, Aristotle viewed friendship which was orientated towards pleasure or usefulness as imperfect, because the motivation was imperfect. Interestingly, Aristotle also taught that friendship with the gods is impossible since they are too remote from human affairs.[5] Although Aristotle portrayed perfect love as something confined to the virtuous elite, he did recognise that *philia* played an important role within the community as a whole, holding the *polis*, the city-state, together.

It was Cicero, the Roman statesman, who exercised the greatest influence on the West's subsequent understanding of friendship. His book on friendship, *De Amicitia*, promoted and popularised many of the same themes that Aristotle had highlighted,[6] for example, that friendship is essential to the fulfilment of human nature in goodness. The full joy and happiness of friendship can only be experienced when we seek it in and for itself, not for any ulterior motive. But the importance of friendship means that it should normally be decided at a mature age, on the basis of a settled likeness in character and interests. Cicero maintained that in a true friend I contemplate a likeness of myself and the love I have towards my friend mirrors the love I have for myself. Friendship is not only essential, it is the most joyful gift of life and those who deprive life of friendship 'seem to take the sun out of the universe'.[7]

Cicero, like many classical writers, saw friendship (*philia* in Greek, *amicitia* in Latin) as superior to both sexual attraction and to familial bonds, since both of these were essential to the furthering of the species. In contrast, friendship had no ulterior purpose. It was not part of our animal nature. It was divine, to be pursued for its own joys and 'goods'.

Reading some of the ancient literature on friendship I am struck by how strange it sounds to modern ears. Sexual intimacy is not ignored or repressed. The ancient worlds of Greece and Rome were certainly not ignorant, ill-informed or naive concerning the many possibilities of sexual ecstasy. To the philosophers and statesmen, *eros* has its place and role but it is a lesser force. The greatest gifts, the greatest joys that life can bring, the true fulfilment of our human nature, all these are to be found in intimate, committed and non-sexual friendships.

Of course, the classical writers were celebrating an idealised conception of bonds between elite males. There is little discussion of friendship between men and women except in marriage, or of friendship between two women. And friendship between people in the lower social orders seemed to be of little significance. (As we will see later, the biblical perspective is dramatically different). But perfect friendship, a mutual attraction which combines both *seeing the good in the other*, and the virtue of *caring for and giving oneself to the other*, represented an ideal which was to exercise a deep influence on the succeeding centuries.

The biblical understanding of friendship has some similarities with that of the classical ideal, but there are many striking differences which we will examine in a later chapter. But for now, I want to ask the question why this classical ideal of friendship was lost over the centuries, and why it should be that for us, living in the twenty-first century, friendship seems both less powerful and less significant than sexual and romantic coupling? Why is it so natural to view the closest and most intimate human relationships through the twin distorting prisms of sex and power?

The changing understanding of the self

The following section may seem rather abstract and philosophical. Why don't we skip the theoretical stuff and fast-forward to the human interest, the stories and anecdotes? Yes, some stories and anecdotes are coming later, but I am convinced that it is not possible to understand our reaction to them, and to see how friendship became so contaminated and laden with suspicion, without engaging with a little of the history of ideas. Here, at the risk of extreme oversimplification, I will give just the broad outlines of the story.

A helpful place to start is to look at the changes taking place in the understanding of the self and what it meant to be human in Europe in the sixteenth and seventeenth centuries. Many historians and philosophers have pointed to a fundamental shift that started around then in the way that many people thought about the world in general and in the way that they thought of themselves.[8] The ancients tended to see the world as having an underlying cosmic order and a meaning that was a given. Everything, including our human nature, was part of the natural order and hence wisdom lay in understanding that cosmic order and trying to live a life that conformed to or was consonant with it. So, when both Aristotle and Cicero argue that a perfect friendship is a fulfilment of our human nature, they understand human nature as a given. What it means to be human is as much an unchangeable part of the natural order as is the sun in the sky.

But in the sixteenth and seventeenth centuries, a new way of seeing the world starts to emerge. Meaning and order is not necessarily inherent in the cosmos. Instead, the world should be seen more like raw material out of which meaning and purpose can be created by each individual. Influential thinkers like René Descartes and Francis Bacon play a key part in this gradual change in seeing, but there is no doubt that disruptive social forces such as the Industrial Revolution and the increasing shift from agrarian to urban societies also play their part.

Starting with Descartes there is a new sense of the importance of the individual. Descartes challenges the classical idea that I can understand myself by understanding the great cosmic order in which I have been placed. Instead, I have to start with *myself* and my own consciousness, my own internal experience. I am 'a thing that thinks' in a society composed of other 'things that think'.[9]

Moving rapidly forward to the nineteenth century, the Enlightenment philosopher John Stuart Mill reinforces the importance of individual choice, autonomy.

> The only purpose for which power can be rightfully exercised over any member of a civilized community against his will, is to prevent harm to others . . . Over himself, over his body and mind, the individual is sovereign.[10]

The wording is significant. There are other sovereigns in the public or political realm, but when it comes to my own private life, my body, my personal morality, what I get up to behind closed doors, in all this I am king, sovereign, absolute master. There is no one who has the right to exercise authority over me. At the time of the Enlightenment, the political concept of the sovereign nation state was being developed. Within the borders of the nation state, the sovereign had complete authority to make whatever laws he wished. Mill extends this understanding to each individual person. Each individual becomes their own nation state with their own sovereign in absolute control. Each person is engaged on an individual 'experiment in living' and no one else has the right to interfere with another's experiment.

It's worth pausing for a moment to reflect on this. We are so familiar with the concepts of liberalism that the strangeness of this atomistic conception of the self and what it implies for human relationships can escape us. It's as though each of us becomes a lonely tyrant, an absolute king, in a small banana republic. Each state can decide to enter into contractual relations with other states, but only by consent and only when the sovereign regards the relationship as being in their own best interests. The most profound, significant and intimate of human bonds starts to be seen as similar to a consensual trading agreement between sovereign countries!

And of course, when you have nation states adjacent to one another you have border disputes. The sovereign has to be perpetually vigilant about his or her borders and guard them, if necessary by force, so as to prevent them being overwhelmed by another state's superior power. My borders extend to the surface of my skin and no one has any right to invade my bodily integrity without my consent. Within this way of thinking, the idea of a genuinely altruistic and self-sacrificial approach to relationships makes no sense at all. Why on earth would you sacrifice your own sovereign concerns to another nation state?

According to this new vision of the self, enlightened self-interest or 'looking after number one' lies at the heart of what it means to be human and at the heart of all human relationships. This understanding of the atomistic individual would have been virtually unimaginable to anyone born prior to the sixteenth century, but to most of us moderns, it seems natural and even self-evident.

Romanticism – express yourself

Descartes had understood the self as an immaterial thinking thing located within a mechanical body. In the seventeenth and early eighteenth centuries, there was a growing emphasis on the materialistic understanding of being human. It is hardly surprising that there was a strong emotional and intellectual backlash against this and the French author Jean-Jacques Rousseau was a key voice in this reaction; a movement which later became known as Romanticism.

Rousseau agrees with Descartes that the identity of the self is formed and preserved in the inner life of the psyche. But not only is the true self to be found through internal reflection, the self can be most true to itself only when all social conventions and restrictions are minimised.

Rousseau imagines a world in which human beings lived simply before any social institutions or conventions emerged, which he calls the 'state of nature'. In such an innocent time human beings had simple desires which could be simply and immediately satisfied. There was no discontinuity or disconnect between what individuals thought or wanted and how they behaved. In contrast, it is society and social conventions that have created the various problems that now afflict human existence.

'Man is born free and everywhere is in chains.'[11] These famous words from the beginning of Rousseau's book, *The Social Contract*, effectively summarised his argument. The individual is at their most authentic before they are shaped (and corrupted) by the need to conform to social conventions.

Rousseau argues that the replacement of the state of nature by the rigid social conventions of eighteenth-century society had devastating consequences on human relationships:

> No more sincere friendships; no more real esteem; no more well-founded trust. Suspicions, offences, fears, coolness, reserve, hatred, betrayal, will constantly hide beneath this even and deceitful veil of politeness, beneath this so much vaunted urbanity which we owe to the enlightenment of our century.[12]

The Romantic movement picked up these themes, arguing that each of us had to find our own way of expressing and living out our identity. If we are to 'find ourselves', it is essential that we refuse to surrender to the pressures to conform being imposed from the outside. And of these destructive pressures, it is particularly the religious authority of the Church and the political authority of the state which must be resisted in the interests of following our own innate desires and finding individual authenticity and self-expression. The person who is truly free is the one who is free to be themselves. And conversely the worst kind of slavery is to be 'living a lie', living in a way which is not authentically consistent with my inner psychological life.

The link between Romanticism and sexual liberation

It's not difficult to see how an emphasis on following one's innate desires and refusing the 'slavery' of conformity to social conventions can lead naturally to a challenge to conventional sexual morality. Increasingly, marriage was seen by the leading Romantic writers as an oppressive social institution restricting free expression of sexual desires. William Godwin, who was the father-in-law of the poet Percy Shelley, wrote that marriage was 'the most odious of all monopolies' because, by making one woman the exclusive property of one man, it creates the context for jealousy, subterfuge and general social corruption. Percy Shelley agreed. 'Love withers under constraint,' he wrote, 'Its very essence is liberty.'[13]

Shelley argued explicitly that marriage could be annulled if the 'pleasurable sensation' became diminished.

If happiness be the object of morality, of all human unions and disunions; if the worthiness of every action is to be estimated by the quantity of pleasurable sensation it is calculated to produce, then the connection of the sexes is so long sacred as it contributes to the comfort of the parties, and is naturally dissolved when its evils are greater than its benefits. There is nothing immoral in this separation.[14]

This passage was written more than two hundred years ago but it is strikingly modern in its sentiment. With the language slightly updated, it would fit in a newspaper article arguing for the removal of all restrictions on no-fault divorce. The traditional idea that marriage is a solemn and lasting covenant which secures and protects the intimate bond between two people has been lost. Now, the marriage is 'sacred' only as long as it causes an excess of 'pleasurable sensations', which is presumably code for sexual and romantic pleasure.

Of course, over the following century, the 'enlightened' views of Shelley and the other Romantics were largely ignored by the majority of the populace. Most people remained in obedient conformity (at least in outward appearance) to the social conventions of monogamy and marital fidelity. It was only a small minority of 'free thinkers' and creative artists who scandalised polite society by their 'liberated' sexual attitudes and behaviour.

And of these, the most notorious promotor of perverse and anarchic sexual freedom was the Marquis de Sade. De Sade was a popular author at the time of the French Revolution, and his books, which celebrated sexual violence, deviant desires and sadomasochistic practices, were popular with revolutionaries who saw a connection between dethroning restrictive sexual conventions and the overthrow of repressive political forces. Both could be seen as an emancipation from tyranny which would allow the individual freedom. Freedom from all forms of restriction and domination. Freedom in the mind and the morals as well as freedom from state oppression.

Of course, De Sade remained strictly a minority interest, and his dangerous books were on the prohibited list. As we have seen, most people continued to live civilised lives of sexual respectability. But the stage had been set for the next earthquake in social attitudes to sexuality, which we will turn to in the next chapter. Enter Sigmund Freud.

2

The sexualisation of friendship and the 'hermeneutic of suspicion'

In the following section I will discuss the distressing subject of historical child sexual abuse. There may, therefore, be some readers who wish to jump ahead to the next section.

As a paediatrician I find the narrative of how Freud came to his theory of infantile sexual fantasy both fascinating and poignant. Sigmund Freud was a highly respectable pillar of Viennese society in the 1890s.[1] He and his cohort of friends and colleagues had no time for the scandalous free thinkers represented by Shelley and the artistic community. He lived a life of middle-class bourgeois respectability, working as a private neurologist. But Freud had developed a novel approach to treating the middle-class patients who came to him with symptoms of neurosis. Instead of first examining his patients and then providing a therapy, Freud asked his patients to recline in comfort on a chaise longue in a darkened, quiet room, devoid of all distractions.[2] He then asked them to talk in detail about everything they had experienced, their symptoms of distress, their dreams, their memories, including everything they could remember from earliest childhood. Freud meanwhile remained silent and unobtrusive, making detailed notes of their words. It was a novel and even revolutionary clinical approach. Many hours were spent with each patient and over several years Freud accumulated a wealth of clinical material. And the results were startling and explosive.

To Dr Freud's surprise, a significant number of patients who came to him with diverse neurological symptoms, especially hysteria and obsessional neurosis, recounted detailed memories of bizarre and traumatic childhood sexual experiences, many of them involving parents or adult family friends. On the evening of 21 April 1896, Sigmund Freud presented a paper before his colleagues at the Society for Psychiatry and Neurology in Vienna, entitled 'The Aetiology of Hysteria'. Using a sample of eighteen patients – male and female – from his practice, he concluded that all of them had been the victims of childhood sexual assaults by an adult. The cause of the patient's distress lay in a trauma inflicted by someone in the child's social circle, often the child's father. The source of internal psychic pain lay in an act inflicted upon the child from outside. This led to what became known, rather misleadingly, as his 'seduction theory'. It was the repressed memories of infantile sexual abuse which had led to the adult neurotic symptoms.

Freud published several scientific papers supporting his theory but there was considerable resistance among his colleagues. He himself had growing doubts. Was it credible that so many children in such a respectable segment of society could have been sexually abused by their parents, particularly their fathers? A year later, in 1897, he published a paper which propounded a new theory and which led on to the birth of psychoanalysis. The patients were not recounting historical episodes of abuse. They were recounting their infantile *sexual fantasies*. Freud had come to the startling conclusion that human infants were intensely sexual beings who were motivated by sexual libido from the earliest months to seek pleasure, strange as this sounds to modern ears.

It took another seventy years before paediatricians began to recognise the reality of child abuse and many people, including myself, think it is highly likely that at least some of Freud's patients had indeed been sexually and physically abused by their fathers and other family members. The cause of their genuine psychological illnesses was not infantile sexual fantasy but childhood sexual abuse. But the tragic truth about what was happening to children in many respectable Viennese families was simply inconceivable to the doctors and therapists of the time. It is only in recent decades that we have been able to acknowledge the terrible reality of child abuse and its long-term psychological consequences.

Strange and offensive as Freud's ideas of childhood sexual development may have been, it is hard to overestimate their impact on Western popular culture. From the perspective of neuroscience and developmental cognitive psychology, Freud's theories have been largely discarded and are generally regarded as scientifically worthless. But his ideas have become part of the zeitgeist, and they have special potency because, as philosopher Roger Scruton once said, they are 'myths that portray themselves as science', and therefore they resist scrutiny and challenge.[3]

The idea that sex in all its forms is good for psychological health, that restriction, control and frustration of sexual drives leads inexorably to mental illness and the breakdown of the personality, that celibacy is a deeply unrealistic and potentially dangerous state, that the impulse for sexual pleasure lies behind much if not all human motivation, initiative and energy, that our very identity is defined by our sexual drives and interests – these seem to be such obvious and scientifically authoritative ideas as to be self-evident and unchallengeable. They are part of the agreed presuppositions of twenty-first-century culture, and they are all traceable to Freud.

It was Freud who first argued that the most noble forms of human activity, including science, art and the 'fiction' of religion, were merely civilised means of ameliorating the unhappiness caused by the frustration of sexual desire. This leads on to the deeply cynical and de-humanising conviction that every act of apparent altruistic concern for others, every demonstration of self-sacrificial love, noble scientific endeavour, artistic creativity and so on, is in fact motivated by a covert desire to find an outlet for sexual frustration! But the individuals themselves are completely unaware (poor fools) of the sexual roots of their behaviour. Here Freud's theories have a brilliant and diabolical twist. 'Ordinary people' persuade themselves that they are acting with altruistic and philanthropic motives. The realisation that all their activities are in fact motivated by sexual frustration would be so unacceptable that the thought must be firmly repressed and banished into the unconscious mind.

Naturally, ordinary people will continue to protest that they are genuinely altruistic and concerned for the welfare of others, and that their religious beliefs are founded on reality. Poor deluded fools. It is only the psychoanalysts and the scientists, the profound seers and visionaries of the modern world, who have insight into the real sexual motivations that lie hidden in the unconscious psyches of the masses.

So here are some of the intellectual roots for the 'hermeneutic of suspicion'. All friendship is sexual because all human behaviour is sexual. How could it be otherwise? Having witnessed the horrors of the First World War, Freud found it necessary to extend his psychoanalytic theories. It was no longer credible that the terrible orgies of destruction that humanity had indulged in from the dawn of time were simply the result of impeded libido, sexual frustration. Freud concluded that there was a second hidden force beside libido that drove all humans and this was 'the drive for death' – a primal, destructive compulsion which expressed itself in a lust to hurt, damage and annihilate. All human behaviour was the result of the constant battle between the desire to unite and the desire to destroy, *Eros* and *Thanatos* (death). This brought a new way of understanding the darker avenues of sexual behaviour explored and celebrated by the Marquis de Sade. Sadism and masochism were the result of *Eros* becoming increasingly mingled with *Thanatos*.

Friedrich Nietzsche

In our historical foray to understand the corruption of friendship, the sexualisation of relationships is not the only story. There is also the question of how relationships became contaminated with ideas of power, control and domination. And here we turn from Freud to the philosopher Friedrich Nietzsche, a key figure in the contemporary obsession with domination, oppression and liberation. Although brought up in a God-fearing, Lutheran household, Nietzsche developed a visceral hatred of Christianity which he saw as the epitome of all that was wrong in civilised society. Christianity taught that you should snivel before God like a worm and plead for forgiveness. Instead, humans should stand up, proud and defiant, free from fear, free from guilt, free from shame – free from all those destructive emotions which were all induced by the evil fiction called religion. Christian compassion for others was the morality of the slave, the doormat, the vanquished. Instead, we should celebrate the great men of humanity, the powerful, the dominant, the *Übermensch*.

Nietzsche's view of morality is particularly significant. 'There are altogether no moral facts. Moral judgement has this in common with religious judgement – that it believes in realities which do not exist.'[4] So Nietzsche provides an essential piece of the jigsaw when it comes to understanding twenty-first-century sexual morality. We don't need to feel guilty about what used to be thought of as sexual 'immorality'. There is no such thing as morality. It doesn't exist. It's a convenient fiction which has been invented and employed by powerful and repressive forces, especially the Church and the state, but also at a smaller scale in the patriarchal family, to control our behaviour and ensure that the interests of the ruling classes are being protected.

Freud taught us how dangerous it was to our mental health to follow sexual conventions. Nietzsche explained that those very conventions were a manipulative fiction created by the strong in order to oppress us. These ideas were taken on and extended by Michel Foucault, one of the most influential thinkers of the twentieth century. Foucault argued that all conventions that decreed that certain sexual practices were unnatural or 'deviant' were in reality tools for legitimising relationships of power and domination. He concludes that all relations between people are affected by the power differences between them. No relationship is free from power and its distortions. But, and very importantly, Foucault argues that the power relations in society are constantly kept hidden and deliberately concealed. The powerful wish to disguise what they are up to. They indulge in a complex charade of creating moral rules, of 'right' and 'wrong', of 'should' and 'should not'. But in order to be liberated we need to see through the charade, we need to unmask the reality. Every claim to truth, to knowledge, to reason, involves power. The individual self is created in the constant interplay between powerful forces – domination and resistance.

What has all this got to do with sexuality? Well, all ideas about sexual relations – whether 'normal' or 'unusual', 'moral' or 'immoral' – are the consequence of power relations in society. Nietzsche says morality is a fiction. But Foucault extends Nietzsche's critique to say, 'look for the power relations'. Morality is created by the powerful. Whenever a person says 'You must not do X' or 'X is wrong', there is an implicit claim to power. They are exerting power over you and you are being dominated, oppressed and bullied. The language of morality is the language of oppression.

Foucault's thought is complex and nuanced and this summary is inevitably simplistic.[5] Nonetheless, it's possible to see the extraordinary influence of his ideas, spreading particularly in academic and university settings since the 1970s, and how they have contributed to a revolution in sexual behaviour. The political vocabulary of 'freedom', 'oppression', 'domination' and 'liberation' has moved out of Marxist agitprop and has become a mainstream way for understanding sexual relationships. The language is now so ubiquitous as to be invisible. But it encapsulates the idea that sex and power are inextricably intertwined in politics, society and human relationships.

Darwin and evolutionary biology

There's one more piece in the jigsaw and that comes from a completely different angle, far away from the abstruse ideas of postmodern philosophy. Charles Darwin had first proposed the idea that human beings were descended from a predecessor of the apes. This had scandalised polite society. There is an apocryphal story that the wife of a bishop on hearing the outrageous idea said, 'My dear, let us hope that it is not true. But if it is, let us hope that it does not become widely known.'

Although the evolutionary mechanism was first proposed by Darwin in *The Descent of Man* published in 1871, it was not until the 1960s that zoologists began undertaking field studies of monkeys and apes. There was an increasing interest in human evolution and in the role of sexual pair bonds. In 1967, the zoologist

Desmond Morris released a book that was to become a bestseller called *The Naked Ape*.[6] He argued that evolutionary forces lay behind the importance of sexuality in human biology. His central claim was that many human sexual prohibitions and preferences could be understood through their biological origins in primate animal behaviour. It wasn't an accident that women desired partners who were monogamous, while men wished to spread their seed to as many women as possible. Hence the most successful males would be those who persuaded their partners that they were being faithful, while in reality they were covertly engaging in promiscuous sex. The Darwinian explanation for our obsession with sex is the survival of the species.

The stage is set for the final act in the great psychodrama of human sexuality: the 1960s and the advent of the sexual liberation movement.

The sixties and the sexual liberation movement

In our journey to explain how friendship became sexualised we have travelled a long way from Aristotle's ideal of virtuous friendship among a small group of social elites. We now come to the final act when abstruse theories about sexuality emerge from the shadows of academic discourse and impact the ordinary lives of billions of people across the planet.

What are the underlying forces which lead to sudden and dramatic changes in popular culture and in common ways of thinking? We've looked briefly at the explosive implications of the ideas of Rousseau, Freud and Nietzsche for subverting conventional sexual morality. But it is not only academics and writers, and the intellectual flow of ideas and theories, that change the way we all think. Sometimes disruptive forces flow from changes in technological inventions, leading to profound and unanticipated shifts in the way that people think and behave. There's no doubt that in the 1960s, the tectonic plates of culture were shifting, but this was not only due to corrosive ideas about sex that had been fomenting for centuries.

A relatively minor pharmaceutical development was going to have dramatic and unexpected consequences – the invention of the oral contraceptive pill.

Of course, contraception had been around since the dawn of civilisation but attempts to limit fertility were generally unreliable, inconvenient and under the control of the man. It was the man who had to use a condom or practise *coitus interruptus* and the female partner was at the mercy of his whims. The fear of pregnancy was a strong barrier to overcome if a woman was to willingly engage in sex outside marriage, and men could use the threat of pregnancy as a means of coercion and control over their partners.

Margaret Sanger was the founder of the American Birth Control League and in 1916 she opened the first birth control clinic in America. She was the driving force behind the search for new and safe contraceptives, and in the 1950s she asked reproductive scientist Gregory Pincus to undertake research into the possibility of a birth control pill. Pincus teamed up with clinician Dr John Rock who was testing the effects of giving the hormone progesterone to his infertile female patients. Funded by private philanthropic money from a wealthy heiress, Pincus and Rock undertook clinical trials in a poor community in Puerto Rico, since, unlike the USA, it had no laws against contraception.[7] The trials showed that the pill was remarkably effective in preventing pregnancy.

In 1957, the FDA (the US drug regulatory authority) approved the use of the first oral pill to 'regulate menstruation'. The package insert warned that the medication had a contraceptive side-effect. By 1959, 500,000 women were ostensibly using it to 'keep their periods regular'. In 1960, the FDA approved the first pill explicitly for use as an oral contraceptive. By 1965, one out of every four married women in America under forty-five had used the medication and by 1967, tens of millions of women around the world were using what was now called 'the pill'.

As many have remarked, the arrival of the contraceptive pill was a watershed moment in sexual relationships between men and women. Now women were in charge. Taken on a daily basis, it was highly effective in preventing pregnancy and it was discreet, undetectable and under the women's sole control. For the first time in the history of humankind, the control of pregnancy was decisively separated from the act of sexual intercourse. Now, at last, it seemed that sex could be free, delightfully spontaneous and consequence-free. During the 1960s, this felt like a huge and revolutionary change for many women and they wrote and talked about it enthusiastically. In particular, many young independent women striving for self-determination and the freedom to pursue their own education and their own interests saw the pill as a means of liberation from patriarchal control. The feminist slogan, 'my body, my choice', said it all.

The contraceptive pill became widely available at a time when many other social forces were changing the dynamics of male–female relationships. Feminism was leading to a rise in women's expectations of equality, education and sexual satisfaction. The permanent and exclusive sexual commitment that marriage involved was increasingly seen as burdensome and restrictive, and divorce laws were being liberalised. Legal abortion became available in many countries.

At the same time, Darwinian ideas of the importance of sex in human evolution were being increasingly popularised and disseminated. Writing in *The Observer*, Robin Dunbar, Professor of Evolutionary Psychology at the University of Oxford, wrote:

> We were all gearing up for the summer of love when, in 1967, Desmond Morris's *The Naked Ape* took us by storm. Its pitch was that humans really were just apes, and much of our behaviour could be understood in terms of animal behaviour and its evolution. Yes, we were naked and bipedal, but beneath the veneer of culture lurked an ancestral avatar . . . In the laid-back, blue-smoke atmosphere of the hippy era, the book struck a chord with the wider public.'[8]

Consumerism

The increasing openness about nudity and sexual references allowed advertisers a new freedom to exploit the commercial potential of sex as a means of selling their products. Discreet sexual themes had been around for decades but now advertisers were discovering the extraordinary effect of explicit sexual imagery in focusing attention and impact. Research showed that sexual arousal elicited by an advert subsequently improved the overall ad evaluation and the chances of future purchase. Market forces led inexorably to increasing use of sexual images and commercial videos featuring explicit sexual behaviour. Sometimes the marketing techniques were more sophisticated, with perfume bottles shaped in suggestive forms and language containing subtle innuendos of sexual desire and consummation. It turned out that sex could be used to sell anything, from cosmetics to power drills, and the research data showed time and again that it worked. Why on earth would any marketer not be using modern persuasive techniques which seemed to tap into the depths of the human psyche?

Welcome to our sex-saturated, sex-obsessed world. The forces unleashed in the 1960s seem to be in full flood more than half a century later and there seems little evidence that a new age of modesty and sexual restraint is about to dawn.

The 'mysticism of the materialist'

It was journalist Malcom Muggeridge who identified a profound truth behind the sexualisation of modern culture. 'Sex is the mysticism of materialism and the only possible religion in a materialistic society... The orgasm has replaced the cross as the focus of longing and fulfilment.'[9]

In a culture that has lost the conviction that there is any transcendent reality beyond the physical reality of the world and of our bodies, sexual longing and the experience of orgasm have come to be seen as the most powerful and 'numinous' experiences that are available to human beings. Some people may find meaning and purpose in art, culture or nature, but to those wedded to materialism these experiences may seem weak and insubstantial. Mystical religious experiences might provide a sense of being caught up out of the world, but these are not open to modern materialists. Sex provides an intensity of experience, of *ec-stasis* (literally, being drawn out of oneself), which surpasses everything else.

Reviewing the journey

At this point it's worth pausing and considering the journey we have made. The ancient world saw *eros* as a powerful but irrational force which could lead to a form of madness. Perfect friendship between elite males was a far more important and satisfying form of human relations. Beginning with Descartes, individualism starts to replace the natural sense of belonging in community. The idea that every person is an isolated sovereign state which makes its own rules and guards its borders gains prominence. Rousseau and the Romantic movement celebrate primal emotional experiences and the need for self-expression in the face of petty social restrictions, like marriage. Darwin explains that humans have evolved from our primate ancestors, and that sexual choices and sexual activity are at the root of our survival as a species. Freud discovers that sexual desire is the concealed motivating force behind our behaviour and that obedience to repressive sexual conventions was the source of most, if not all, mental illness. Nietzsche and Foucault reveal that all conventional moral rules are cleverly concealed tools to enable the powerful to suppress the population. The language of sexual morality is revealed as the language of oppression and whenever a person says, 'You must not sleep with X' or 'Your kind of sexual behaviour is deviant', in reality you are being dominated and bullied by patriarchal and abusive forces. Add in the contraceptive pill, the power of sex in a capitalist economy and the idea that orgasms put you in touch with the meaning of life, and you have our sex-saturated, confused and suspicious world.

Of course, the brief narrative I have presented over the last two chapters is a highly oversimplified caricature of a complex shifting panorama of ideas. There are many subtleties, nuances and complexities which the academic social historian or philosopher would wish to interpose. But the basic outlines remain. The extraordinary changes we have witnessed in personal and sexual behaviour over the last decades can be traced to a confluence of deep forces and ideas going back centuries.

The hermeneutic of suspicion

Philosopher Paul Ricoeur was the first to describe Marx, Freud and Nietzsche as the three 'masters of suspicion'.[10] As academic Rita Felski subsequently put it, the three 'share a commitment to unmasking "the lies and illusions of consciousness"; they are the architects of a distinctively modern style of interpretation that circumvents obvious or self-evident meanings in order to draw out less visible and less flattering truths'.[11] The phrase 'the hermeneutic of suspicion', using the academic term for interpretation of a literary text, has been employed to describe this critical stance towards the world. When applied to literary interpretation it is a way of reading texts 'against the grain' and 'between the lines'. It involves highlighting and cataloguing what is not said and laying bare the contradictions in the text. The hermeneutic of suspicion doesn't ask 'what does this text mean?' but rather 'what is it hiding?'[12]

When applied to human relationships, the hermeneutic of suspicion is a helpful term to describe our modern unwillingness to accept that relationships are what they appear to be on the surface. In particular, don't trust what people say about their relationships and above everything else don't be naive. Read between the lines, look for ulterior motives, identify the power dynamics, the manipulative intent and the sexual subscript. They are bound to be there, even if they have been carefully disguised to throw people off the scent. The only way to survive in the world is to be intensely suspicious and distrustful of those who claim to be behaving innocently and altruistically. Much better to stick with people who are overt about their selfishness and self-centred preoccupations. The people to be suspicious of are those who claim to be genuinely caring, those who seem to be offering themselves to you without an obviously selfish motive. After all, 'There's no such thing as a free lunch.'

And so, we come to this historical moment of suspicion and mistrust. We cannot underestimate the incalculable damage done to Christian friendship by the litany of abuse scandals implicating highly respected and prominent Christian leaders, coming from every wing of the Christian church. It turns out that the 'masters of suspicion' were not completely wrong. Sometimes it pays to be suspicious. We are now much more aware than we used to be that while it may be possible to develop healthy Christian friendships, the powerful hidden forces of sex and emotional coercion, control and manipulation are capable of distorting and ultimately destroying intimate relationships within the Christian community.

As we will discuss in greater detail in a later chapter, we must take full account of the painful and damaging examples of the abuse of power, of exploitation, predatory sexual activities, the abuse of vulnerable individuals and unbelievable public hypocrisy.

But now we turn to the biblical material. How does a biblical perspective illuminate and challenge the contemporary confusion about human relationships providing a compelling, rich and wonderfully attractive vision of what friendship can be? I have grown to see that there is a profound connection between the gospel and human friendship. The gospel, the good news about Jesus, concerns the re-creation and renewal of everything and everyone for communion, through the person and sacrifice of Christ. And the deepest and most intimate friendships between Christian believers can become a living embodiment and tangible enactment of the restoration of communion between broken human beings which the gospel enables.

3
Friendship in the Bible

Friendship seems such an important and central part of Christian living and yet as I started my research for this book I was immediately struck by the relative dearth of recent thoughtful and scholarly engagement with the biblical material about friendship.[1] When one thinks about the wealth of writing, research and sermonising on the Bible's teaching about sexual relationships and about marriage, the lack of attention to friendship as a central topic in human relationships seems extraordinary. Is it possible that many modern biblical scholars, exegetes and church leaders have unwittingly been influenced by the same obsession with sex that characterises our culture, leading to a relative disregard for non-sexual friendship?

Yet once one starts to look at the Scriptures, it is immediately obvious that there is a wealth of material about friendship in both the Old and New Testaments. And it is also immediately obvious that the biblical narrative frames and understands friendship in very different ways from the classical Greek and Roman ideals.

Friendship in the Old Testament

The Hebrew Bible has a range of words and idioms for friendship which reflect the complexity of the underlying relationships. Although the biblical text has no word for the abstract concept 'friendship', there are a number of different words used for 'friend'. The most common word is *rea'*, which is a rather general and neutral word, also translated as 'neighbour'. But there are many other Hebrew words such as *ōhēb*, literally 'one who loves'; *allûp*, which may be related to a word meaning 'gentle'; and *mĕyuddā*, 'one who is known (to me)'.[2]

The biblical narrative has a special place for the intense, intimate bond of love and loyalty that may develop between two people. Proverbs 18:24 says 'a man of many companions [*rea'*] may come to ruin but there is a friend [*ōhēb*] who sticks [*dabeq*] closer than a brother' and *dabeq* means literally to cling. For instance, *dabeq* is the word used in the famous passage about marriage in Genesis 2:24 'Therefore a man shall leave his father and his mother and hold fast [*dabeq*] to his wife.'

So, the passage in Proverbs 18:24 makes a clear contrast between multiple superficial acquaintances on the one hand and, on the other hand, the intimate soulmate who sticks, holds on, adheres. In an ancient Middle Eastern culture, family relationships were regarded as of crucial significance and importance. So, it is very striking and significant that in this passage in Proverbs, there is celebration for the friend whose closeness exceeds even the closest family bond.

The same word *dabeq* is used of Ruth 'clinging' to Naomi (in Ruth 1:14). In Deuteronomy 13:6, an especially intimate companion is described as 'your friend who is as your own soul' (Deuteronomy 13:6) and Jonathan's soul (*nephesh*) was said to be 'bound' or 'knit' to the soul of David using another Hebrew word (*niqšĕrâ*) implying binding and tying (1 Samuel 18:1).

I have no choice about many of the relationships in which I am locked. My family, my relatives, my kinspeople, my neighbours, my tribe. All these are unchosen, part of the givens of my life in community. But my special friend is a *chosen one*, the one I have chosen to trust, to love, to cling to and to bind my soul with. And in the closest and most significant of friendships, when I bind my soul to my friend, I take on a solemn and binding covenant commitment to them.

A recurring theme in both the book of Psalms and the book of Proverbs is that true friends are trustworthy and loyal – and, in particular, the fact that a true friend will not repay good with evil. Hence the betrayal of trust between friends is especially painful and shocking, as David laments in Psalm 55:

For it is not an enemy who taunts me –
then I could bear it;

it is not an adversary who deals insolently with me –
    then I could hide from him.
But it is you, a man, my equal,
    my companion, my familiar friend.
We used to take sweet counsel together.
(Psalm 55:12–14)

The same theme of betrayal of friendship is found in Psalm 41:9 'Even my close friend in whom I trusted, who ate my bread, has lifted his heel against me.'

True friends will speak honestly even if this causes real pain, 'Faithful are the wounds of a friend' (Proverbs 27:6) and the clash of opinions between friends can be productive, 'Iron sharpens iron, and one man sharpens another' (Proverbs 27:17). And deep friendship has a special significance at times of suffering and hardship, 'A friend loves at all times, and a brother is born for adversity' (Proverbs 17:17).

The friendships we develop have powerful influences on our lives – for good or evil. And so, our choice of friends is of crucial significance. 'The righteous choose their friends carefully, but the way of the wicked leads them astray' (Proverbs 12:26 NIV). If we choose to walk with the wise we will become wise ourselves, but 'the companion of fools will suffer harm' (Proverbs 13:20).

The Old Testament views the most significant friendships as representing a voluntarily chosen bond of extraordinary closeness and covenant loyalty. And, in a theme we will return to below, the deepest kind of covenant friendship reflects the very character of God himself. The word *chesed*, often translated as 'steadfast love', 'covenant love' or 'loyal love' is one of the foundational aspects of the character of YHWH.[3] It is how God himself chooses to define himself, 'The LORD, the LORD, a God merciful and gracious, slow to anger, abounding in steadfast love [*chesed*] and faithfulness [*emet*]' (Exodus 34:6). Intimate, committed and loyal friendships between followers of YHWH are intended to model, reflect, be indwelt with and energised by the very *chesed* of God himself.

These themes are modelled in two paradigm friendships in the Old Testament. Both are depicted as extraordinarily intimate and committed relationships – patterns of supreme and sacrificial friendship. They are, of course, the relationships between Ruth and Naomi and between David and Jonathan. In both cases the friendships are unexpected and counter-intuitive; they are an unpredictable and unanticipated development in the narrative. But strikingly, both these friendships come to play a crucial role in the plot-line of the Old Testament, since they both contribute to the Davidic line of inheritance which culminates in the birth of Jesus of Nazareth.

Ruth and Naomi

The friendship of Ruth and Naomi has its roots in the dutiful relationship between mother-in-law and daughter-in-law. Driven by famine, Naomi had travelled with her husband and two sons from Bethlehem into the alien land of Moab. The sons had both taken Moabite wives, Orpah and Ruth, but then disaster had struck the family. First Naomi's husband died. It seems that Naomi had managed to secure wives for her two sons but then both the sons had died, leaving a trio of widows attempting to survive by their wits. The implications were dire. Without any adult male to protect them, and given the lawless conditions of the time, the three widows were facing a perilous existence. At any moment they could be raped or abused by a stranger, coerced into a disastrous relationship, or they might face starvation and destitution through lack of a bread-winner. It was no surprise that in the Old Testament law, widows were repeatedly singled out (along with orphans and immigrants) as particularly vulnerable and hence worthy of special protection.

Naomi hears that the famine has lifted in the land of Judah and decides to return there to her home people. But she realises that there is no future in Judah for her two daughters-in-law. Their best chance lay in staying in Moab and hoping for remarriage to a Moabite man. It is clear from the narrative that Naomi, out of love and concern for the two younger women, is deliberately releasing her daughters-in-law from their binding familial duties to look after her.

Go, return each of you to her mother's house. May the LORD
[YHWH] deal kindly with you, as you have dealt with the dead
and with me. May the LORD [YHWH] grant that you find rest
each of you in the house of her husband.
(Ruth 1:8–9)

The best hope for both women is remarriage in the land of Moab.

Orpah understands the reality of the situation and after a tearful
farewell she returns 'to her people and to her gods' (v 15). The
narrative is clear about the spiritual dimension of the women's
decisions. Naomi invokes the blessing of YHWH on the women. But
although Orpah had been married to a Hebrew man, she was now
returning to the worship of the pagan Moabite gods, of whom
one was Chemosh, described in 1 Kings 11 as 'the abomination
of Moab'.

Orpah gives Naomi a farewell kiss and leaves but, unexpectedly
and astonishingly, Ruth refuses to abandon Naomi and instead
clings to her (v 14), described by the narrator with the powerful
Hebrew word *dabeq*. Ruth clings on, despite Naomi's gentle
persuasion for her to leave, and utters a solemn vow of covenant
commitment to Naomi, to her people and to her God.

Do not urge me to leave you or to return from following you.
For where you go I will go, and where you lodge I will lodge.
Your people shall be my people, and your God my God. Where
you die I will die, and there will I be buried.
(Ruth 1:16–17)

Ruth refuses to follow the reasonable, rational and culturally
appropriate choice that Orpah has made. There was a good chance
that she could find a new husband in Moab. Her decision to bind
herself to Naomi must have been founded on something other than
self-interest or some expectation of future material blessing from
following Naomi's God. All she had witnessed in the family she had
joined was two weddings and three funerals! As Chris Wright put
it, it's a striking example of an 'unprosperity gospel'.[4]

By committing herself to Naomi, Ruth was committing herself to the faith of Israel and to Israel's God. So what was it that Ruth had witnessed in this little blighted Israelite family that led her to commit herself to their God, YHWH? Chris Wright comments that 'There is something Abrahamic about this. Even in famine-induced exile, Israelites have become a blessing to a foreign woman.' Ruth becomes a model of a faithful Gentile who through covenantal friendship with a believing Jewish widow is caught up into God's deeper salvation purposes.[5]

Ruth's friendship with Naomi led to great personal risks for both of them. It's not even clear that at first Naomi welcomed her daughter-in-law's fervent expression of devotion. The text implies that Naomi stopped talking to Ruth after she refused to return with Orpah! Naomi may have been wondering how she would be treated in Bethlehem when she returned with this young foreign widow in tow. Her next words in the text show that bitterness is her dominant emotion. 'I went away full, and the LORD [YHWH] has brought me back empty' (Ruth 1:21). Well, not quite. God has given her a remarkably persevering daughter-in-law who won't go away![6]

And so the narrative continues. Despite such unpromising beginnings, the destitution of their circumstances and their lowly social status, Naomi and Ruth form an indissoluble bond of mutual assistance and intimate support. So what can we learn from this remarkable and unexpected development in the narrative?

First, there is a clear distinction between the loyalty and care that we owe to our family members, to our blood relatives, our kin, on the one hand, and intimate, committed friendship on the other. Our family relationships are given to us, but our friendships are based on *free choice*. Ruth had fulfilled her familial duties to Naomi, she was free to walk away. But now she *chooses* instead to cling to Naomi and to take upon herself a solemn and binding vow of lifelong loyalty.

Second, the friendship is both *intergenerational* and *interracial*. Instead of the classical Greek and Roman ideal of a friendship between social equals, Ruth and Naomi show how an intimate, committed and lifelong friendship can transcend barriers of age, culture and race. Of course, they share common commitments to one another and, above all, to the service of the living God, but it is clear that their *differences* are part of the unusual chemistry between them.

Third, the friendship combines deep love and intimacy with *practical and mutual caring* for the needs of the other. Ruth takes on the role of obtaining food for both women, Naomi provides advice for Ruth on Israeli cultural practices around harvesting, how to minimise the risk of being attacked and how to negotiate the delicate task of approaching Boaz as her kinsman redeemer. But Chris Wright points out that again she disobeys her mother-in-law. Naomi had helpfully told Ruth precisely what she should do: 'go and uncover his feet and lie down, and he will tell you what to do' (Ruth 3:4). But when the moment comes, Ruth departs from the script. 'Spread your wings over your servant, for you are a redeemer' (v 9). In other words, 'Marry me!'

The intimacy and significance of Ruth and Naomi's relationship is well known to the women of the village. 'Your daughter-in law who loves you, who is more to you than seven sons, has given birth to [a son]' (Ruth 4:15). In the culture of the time, to have given birth to seven sons was the utmost height of maternal bliss and fulfilment, but Ruth's friendship and love mean more to Naomi even than this.

Fourth, intimate committed friendship can have *wonderful and unanticipated consequences*. In the sparse wording of the narrative is hidden a depth of love, tenderness and unexpected joy. 'Then Naomi took the child and laid him on her lap and became his nurse. And the women of the neighbourhood gave him a name, saying "A son has been born to Naomi"' (Ruth 4:16–17).

Naomi has a grandson to cherish in her old age and there's no doubt that this child would be doubly precious – so unexpected and so loved. The extraordinarily special child who had been born to the one person who was more to her than seven sons. Ruth enters the Davidic line and the lowly Moabite woman becomes one of the heroines of the faith. Jesus himself is descended from Ruth (Matthew 1:5), and the friendship of Ruth and Naomi is celebrated throughout the subsequent history of Israel and provides a model for us nearly 3,000 years later.

David and Jonathan

David and Jonathan's friendship on the surface seems very different from Naomi and Ruth's. Jonathan was one of the elite, a proven warrior and leader, the oldest son of Saul and heir to the throne. At the time he first met David, Jonathan was probably in his thirties and at the peak of his military prowess. David was a young upstart from a poor peasant family, a mere shepherd boy and no more than eighteen. David had been ignored by his father and older brothers, and yet had had the temerity to take on the mighty Goliath and vanquish him with what could have seemed like a cunning peasant trick. Jonathan could easily have seen him both as unfit to be his friend and a potential rival for the throne. As one commentator put it 'When Jonathan went to meet David he had nothing to gain and everything to lose'.[7]

What was worse, although Jonathan appeared eminently qualified for kingship, his father's failure as king meant that Jonathan's claim to the throne was to be negated. The prophet Samuel had stated as much in his public condemnation of Saul:

> You have not kept the command of the LORD your God, with which he commanded you. For then the LORD would have established your kingdom over Israel forever. But now your kingdom shall not continue. The LORD has sought a man after his own heart, and the LORD has commanded him to be prince over his people.
> (1 Samuel 13:13–14)

Jonathan might have been expected to be bitter and self-pitying. But his immediate response to his young rival David was one of generosity:

> Saul said to him, 'Whose son are you, young man?' And David answered, 'I am the son of your servant Jesse the Bethlemite.'
>   As soon as he had finished speaking to Saul, the soul of Jonathan was knit [Hebrew *nikšĕrâ*] to the soul of David, and

Jonathan loved him as his own soul. And Saul took him that day and would not let him return to his father's house. Then Jonathan made a covenant with David because he loved him as his own soul. And Jonathan stripped himself of the robe that was on him and gave it to David, and his armour, and even his sword and bow and belt.
(1 Samuel 17:58 – 18:4)

Jonathan's generous friendship leads him to strip himself of his royal robes and all the trappings of a mighty warrior, and give them to his beloved David. To wear the royal robes and armour was a supreme privilege for anybody but it was especially remarkable and socially inappropriate to give it to someone of David's peasant heritage and lowly status. Jonathan's desire was clearly to remove all the evidence of David's shepherd-boy origins and to elevate him immediately to the status of royal prince. Then they could stand side by side as social equals.

There is also symbolic significance in Jonathan stripping himself of his armour. He was deliberately making himself defenceless and vulnerable. He was putting himself into the hands of his new-found friend who was also his rival. There can be no deep friendship without risk and no love without vulnerability. When we open our lives and our hearts to another, we are making ourselves vulnerable to rejection and hurt. Jonathan makes (literally 'cuts' – Hebrew *krt*) a solemn covenant with David out of his intense love. What was it that drew Jonathan instantaneously to this young peasant boy? Fyodor Dostoevsky wrote, 'To love a person means to see him as God intended him to be.'[8]

Some years later, Saul is trying every means to kill David who is on the run. David meets Jonathan secretly. At this point in their friendship, David's life is in intense jeopardy and Jonathan's actions could mean life or death for him. David reminds him of their original covenant-making and of its foundation in God himself. 'Therefore deal kindly [literally 'show *chesed*'] with your servant, for you have brought your servant into a covenant of the LORD [YHWH] with you' (1 Samuel 20:8).

In response to David's urgent request, Jonathan renews his lifelong covenant of loyalty and protection to David, but he also recognises that if God's purposes are going to be fulfilled and David becomes king, then Jonathan's own life will be at risk. When the usurper finally gained the throne, it was standard practice to slaughter immediately all the legitimate heirs of the vanquished king. Jonathan would be powerless before the murderous intent of the new ruler.

So, Jonathan's words have a desperate urgency:

May the LORD [YHWH] be with you as he has been with my father. If I am still alive show me the steadfast love [*chesed*] of the LORD [YHWH] that I may not die, and do not cut off your steadfast love [*chesed*] from my house forever, when the LORD [YHWH] cuts off every one of the enemies of David from the face of the earth. And Jonathan made a covenant with the house of David saying, 'May the LORD [YHWH] take vengeance on David's enemies.' And Jonathan made David swear again by his love for him, for he loved him as he loved his own soul. (1 Samuel 20:13–17).

God's *chesed* is intermingled with – underpins, empowers and authenticates – the *chesed* that David and Jonathan express in their covenant of loyal love. And, of course, this is much more than mere words. Their *chesed*, expressed in solemn words and oaths, then becomes the foundation, the touchstone, of their actions as both of them willingly risk their lives for the other.

Once it became apparent that there was no possibility of a reconciliation between David and Saul, and that David must go his own way, the parting of the covenant friends is described in poignant words. Given the desperate nature of the war in Israel, they did not know whether they would see one another again.

As soon as the boy had gone, David rose from beside the stone heap and fell on his face to the ground and bowed three times. And they kissed one another and wept with one another, David weeping the most. Then Jonathan said to David, 'Go in peace, because we have sworn both of us in the name of the LORD [YHWH], saying, 'The LORD [YHWH] shall be between me and you, and between my offspring and your offspring, forever.' And he rose and departed, and Jonathan went into the city. (1 Samuel 20:41–42)

They reaffirm to one another that their bond is not based on human attraction alone, but on the name of YHWH. The covenant between David and Jonathan is bound up with the everlasting covenant of God himself with his people.

A final highly risky and clandestine meeting in the wilderness between the covenant friends is recorded in 1 Samuel 23:15–18 (NIV):

While David was at Horesh in the Desert of Ziph, he learned that Saul had come out to take his life. And Saul's son Jonathan went to David at Horesh and helped him find strength in God. 'Don't be afraid,' he said. 'My father Saul will not lay a hand on you. You will be king over Israel, and I will be second to you. Even my father Saul knows this.' The two of them made a covenant before the LORD [YHWH]. Then Jonathan went home, but David remained at Horesh.

The Hebrew says in literal translation that Jonathan 'strengthened his hand through (or in) God'. Jonathan is motivated by a deep loyalty to God and to his hidden purposes. He recognises that David is central to God's plans and purposes for the entire nation of Israel and he encourages and strengthens David in his commitment to be God's person and to depend utterly on God's power and leading. I come back to those profound words of Dostoevsky, 'To love a person means to see him as God intended him to be.'

The spiritual strengthening that Jonathan's covenantal friendship achieved for David, enabled David later to do the same for himself, when confronted with catastrophic failure and danger. In 1 Samuel 30:6 exactly the same phrase is used, 'And David was greatly distressed for the people spoke of stoning him, because all the people were bitter in soul, each for his sons and daughters. But David strengthened himself in the LORD [YHWH] his God.'[9]

Despite being apparent rivals they shared a deep and common interest in fulfilling God's purposes in their lives. 'You will be king over Israel and I shall be for you as second.' Jonathan repeats his renunciation of his right to the throne in order to support God's purposes for David. And again, they express their covenant commitment in words of loyalty to one another. They solemnly enact or 'cut' a covenant before YHWH to express to one another again that they were placing their lives and futures together in God's purposes.

An important yardstick to assess the deepest friendships is whether they are encouraging spiritual growth and greater dependency on God. Does this friendship genuinely express the nature of God's *chesed*? Is it encouraging and realising God's purpose and potential in the other person's life, even if this means that I may be sidelined and take the lower place? 'I shall be for you as second.'

Jesus' words in John 15:13 act as a solemn commentary on Jonathan's actions 'Greater love has no one than this, that someone lay down his life for his friends.' And indeed, Jonathan's *chesed* does eventually lead him to lay down his life, protecting David both from the murderous jealousy of Saul, Jonathan's father, and from the Amalekites. And David's heart is torn out:

> Jonathan lies slain on your heights.
> I grieve for you, Jonathan my brother;
>   you were very dear to me.
> Your love for me was wonderful,
>   more wonderful than that of women.
> (2 Samuel 1:25 NIV)

It's a painful reminder that the loyal love that God calls us to with a few covenant friends always carries a painful cost. As C. S. Lewis put it:

> To love at all is to be vulnerable. Love anything and your heart will be wrung and possibly broken. If you want to make sure

of keeping it intact you must give it to no one, not even an animal . . . To love is to be vulnerable.[10]

A single woman recently told me of her deep covenant friendship with another young woman, founded on their profound shared commitment to Christ and to cross-cultural mission. When her friend died at a young age from cancer, she was devastated and grieving. But the intensity of her grief seemed to have been met with incomprehension by her colleagues. 'She was only a friend. It wasn't as though you have lost a husband or close relative.' It seems that there is a strange unwillingness in our culture to recognise or celebrate the life-changing significance of our deepest friendships, and the depth of the pain that separation can bring.

The modern hermeneutic of suspicion says that there must have been a sexual element in the love between David and Jonathan. Surely Dr Freud has some insights to contribute here. It's simply not credible that two men could have such an intimate and passionate relationship without there being a homoerotic element.

The Jewish nation was well aware of the reality of homosexual practices in the surrounding nations. But the Levitical law had explicitly described homosexual activities between men as an abomination (Leviticus 18:22, 20:13). It's pretty clear that David has strong heterosexual desires and his adulterous relationship with Bathsheba leads to a self-excoriating sense of sin and guilt:

> For I know my transgressions
>   and my sin is always before me.
> Against you, you only have I sinned . . .
>
> Cleanse me with hyssop, and I will be clean . . .
>
> Do not cast me from your presence
>   or take your Holy Spirit from me.
> (Psalm 51:3–11 NIV)

Given the cultural assumptions of the time, it is surely beyond credulity that David and Jonathan's relationship, which was described as a covenant founded on the *chesed* of God, was in reality based on what would have been regarded at the time as an illicit sexual attraction. As far as I am aware, not one of the ancient or modern biblical commentators raised this possibility until Freudian ideas entered the culture in the early twentieth century.

We have seen in the remarkable biblical accounts of the two paradigm relationships, Ruth and Naomi, David and Jonathan, how intimate, committed and loyal friendships between followers of YHWH are intended to model, reflect, be indwelt with and energised by the covenant love, the *chesed* of God himself. Indeed, this is surely one aspect of our creation in God's image. We are called to reflect God's very nature and being in the deep, mysterious and wonderful bonds we create with one another.

We will return to this theme of how human friendships are intended to model, reflect and mediate the love of God in a later chapter. But for now, we turn to the wonderful concept of friendship with God himself.

Friendship with God

It is worth pausing for a moment to consider what an extraordinary concept this is. The word 'friendship' seems too prosaic, even banal, to describe an approach to the awesome, all-powerful, numinous and mysterious Source of the Cosmos. There is a risk of trivialisation and sentimentality as we contemplate the idea of friendship with God. As though the Almighty might be a cosy and tolerant companion whom we may add to the list of our human friends.

Certainly, it is hard to conceive of friendship as a suitable word for any other gods of world history. Friendship with Allah would be blasphemous, friendship with Plato's Form of the Good or Aristotle's Unmoved Mover would be simply absurd. And yet the God of the Bible characterises himself as one who seeks friendship with those pathetic groundlings, those whom he has created for intimacy and into whom he has breathed his Spirit.

Perhaps one of the earliest hints of this can be seen in the striking passage in Genesis 2 when God breathes into the nostrils of Adam.

In the Genesis creation narratives, the creation of all the other living beings is described in merely passive terms. 'Let the earth bring forth living creatures' (Genesis 1:24). But the formation of Adam is described in very different language: 'then the LORD God formed the man of dust from the ground and breathed into his nostrils the breath of life, and the man became a living creature' (Genesis 2:7). The imagery suggests the face-to-face intimacy of a kiss between the Creator God and the lowly being that has been crafted out of the dust of the ground.

It has often been said that in the Genesis creation narratives, everything created by God was described as good. There was just one thing that was said to be 'not good' and that was the aloneness of Adam. As Tim Keller put it, 'Adam was not lonely because he was imperfect, but because he was perfect.'[11] So the ache for human intimacy, the ache for friendship, for companionship, is not the result of sin and brokenness. We have been created in such a way that we cannot even enjoy paradise without human friends. As Mark Labberton put it, the longing for communion and for intimacy is rooted in our nature. 'Before communion is gospel, it is primal. A longing for intimacy that is not about bodily appetite . . . Friendship is an embodied enactment of the restoration of communion.'[12] And in his love and grace, God provides the ideal companion for Adam in the person of Eve, so that they can enjoy the garden together. Of course, the creation of Eve is not solely intended to solve Adam's aloneness! The Genesis narrative is clear that it is man and woman *together* who are created in God's image and who are *jointly* given the creation mandates to fill the earth and subdue it (Genesis 1:27–28).

In the subsequent narrative, the Creator is depicted coming to his wonderful garden in order to pass the time with his beloved friends, 'walking in the garden in the cool of the day' (Genesis 3:8–9). It's a beautiful and strangely commonplace image of friendship. There seems to be no ulterior motive. This is not a business appointment or a strategy meeting to work out how the human couple are going to fulfil their creation mandates. It is simply the Creator wanting to spend time with his dear friends, to enjoy the sounds and fragrances of the evening together. In the US slang, he just wants to 'hang out' with them. And his poignant call 'Where are you?' reveals his moving grief at the sudden and catastrophic rupture of intimacy that their actions caused.

The metaphor of friends walking together recurs through the biblical narrative. And in the continuing storyline of the Old Testament there are a small number of extraordinary individuals who are described as having recaptured some of the prelapsarian intimacy with God that Adam and Eve had lost. Enoch 'walks with God' for the long years of his life, and such is the closeness of his friendship with God that 'he was not, for God took him' (Genesis 5:24). Just as Enoch walked with God, so God chooses to walk among his people, 'I will walk among you and will be your God, and you shall be my people' (Leviticus 26:12).

Abraham repeatedly demonstrates his covenant loyalty to YHWH – and his deep closeness and faith-filled obedience leads to God choosing to share his plans and purposes about the coming judgement of Sodom, 'Shall I hide from Abraham what I am about to do? . . .For I have known him' (Genesis 18:17, 19, literal translation). The Hebrew word for 'known' is *yd'*, implying a deep and intimate communion. Abraham never forgets his fragility and weakness as he speaks to God. 'Behold I have undertaken to speak to the Lord, I who am but dust and ashes' (Genesis 18:27). But his extraordinary familiarity and closeness with God gives him the temerity to engage in what could almost be described as horse-trading over the impending judgement of Sodom! And God himself, through the words of the prophet Isaiah, later describes Abraham as 'my friend'. 'But you Israel, my servant, Jacob whom I have chosen, the offspring of Abraham, my friend' (Isaiah 41:8).

Moses too is described in the same terms of intimacy, communion and trust, as one with whom God shared his heart. Chris Wright points out that in Exodus 32 – 34, Moses effectively rebukes God for even thinking of destroying the children of Israel and proposing to start again with 'the children of Moses'. Moses engages in some fairly robust negotiation until God 'gives way' and agrees that he will dwell in the midst of the people. It's almost as though God says, 'Well, OK, if that's what you really want, let's do this your way.' There is a certain vulnerability and integrity on both sides in this remarkable exchange.[13] And so it is especially significant that this kind of relationship is described by the anonymous narrator as friendship. 'The LORD [YHWH] used to speak to Moses face to face, as a man speaks to his friend' (Exodus 33:11). Moses, like Abraham, is fully known by God, again using the Hebrew root, *yd'*: 'I know you by name.' And despite his temerity, Moses is delighted in by God: 'and you have also found favour in my sight' (Exodus 33:12).

Although David is not described explicitly as a 'friend of God', the intimacy and closeness of his unique relationship with God are self-evident throughout the Davidic psalms:

> Whom have I in heaven but you?
> > And there is nothing on earth that I desire besides you.
> My flesh and my heart may fail,
> > but God is the strength of my heart and my portion
> > > forever.
> (Psalm 73:25–26)

> How precious to me are your thoughts, God!
> > How vast is the sum of them!
> Were I to count them,
> > they would outnumber the grains of sand –
> > when I awake, I am still with you.
> (Psalm 139:17–18 NIV)

> You make known to me the path of life;
> > you will fill me with joy in your presence,
> > with eternal pleasures at your right hand.
> (Psalm 16:11 NIV)

Friendship in the New Testament

The Hebraic model of deep and intimate friendship continues into the New Testament, but it takes on novel and surprising forms.

Above all else, it is in the behaviour and practices of Jesus of Nazareth that we see new aspects of friendship. It is Jesus who subverts traditional Hebraic cultural and rabbinic practice and attitudes by his extraordinary behaviour.

As we have seen, friendship between social equals was celebrated by classical Greek and Roman authors. But deep and intimate non-sexual friendship between an older and younger man was unusual. Both Jewish and Greek models of training and discipling were deeply hierarchical, formal and boundaried. The Greek philosophers had their disciples (*mathetes*), who were often enrolled in formal schools such as Plato's Academy in Athens. Their role was close to that of modern university students. They had to listen to extended lectures, discourses and interrogations from the Master, often given over many years. They had to write down notes from the Master's teaching. And their ultimate goal was that the student might themselves become the next Master, so that knowledge could be passed on to the next generation. It was a formal, intellectual and technical exercise.

In first-century Judaism, there was also a well-established teacher–disciple relationship. The teacher was addressed as 'Rabbi' derived from the Hebrew *rby* ('my great one') and the title expressed considerable respect. A saying attributed to Rabbi Elazar ben Shammua (AD 130–160) was, 'Let the fear of your teacher be as the fear of heaven.'[14] The rabbi's role was to instruct his disciples both through his words and his behaviour. He was responsible for protecting them from harm and providing for their needs. In return, the disciples assumed the role of faithful followers, including the performance of menial tasks and the perpetuation of their Master's teaching.

It is clear that Jesus accepted the title of 'Rabbi' from his disciples. Indeed, in John 13:13, he emphasises his divine authority over them: 'You call me Teacher [*didaskolos*] and Lord [*kyrios*], and you are right, for so I am.' But Jesus makes this statement of his status and authority in the context of the dramatic and shocking act of washing his disciples' feet, which no Jewish rabbi would ever have contemplated.

And it is striking that Jesus explicitly discouraged his disciples from appropriating the title or the hierarchical customs of first-century rabbis.

> But you are not to be called rabbi, for you have one teacher, and you are all brothers. And call no man your father on earth, for you have one Father, who is in heaven. Neither be called instructors [*kathegetes*], for you have one instructor, the Christ. The greatest among you shall be your servant. Whoever exalts himself will be humbled, and whoever humbles himself will be exalted.
> (Matthew 23:8–12)

Jesus' teaching is remarkable in its historical context. The contemporary Jewish practice was that a student, after several years of training with his teacher, earned the right to be addressed as 'Rabbi', so that he could recruit his own followers. But it seems clear that Jesus was explicitly warning against this model of discipleship among his followers. There was only one Rabbi, one Teacher, one Instructor and one Lord. And the paradoxical model of leadership that Jesus taught, and then exemplified in his own life, was one of sacrificial service, laying down one's life for the flock.

But it is in the well-known passage in John 15, set in the context of the Upper Room discourses, that Jesus most obviously subverts the traditional rabbinic role. It is notable that Judas Iscariot had left the group, immediately after the foot-washing episode and before Jesus opens his heart to the remaining eleven:

> I no longer call you servants [Greek *doulos*], because a servant does not know his master's business. Instead, I have called you friends [Greek *philos*], for everything that I learned from my Father I have made known to you.
> (John 15:15 NIV)

As many commentators have pointed out this construction 'no longer . . . instead' reflects a climactic moment in salvation history.

In the old covenant, God's people were his servants. But now, although the title servant or bond-slave [Greek *doulos*] is still used of Christians, we are more than servants. We have become friends!

The essence of friendship with Jesus is self-disclosure and vulnerability, that deep and intimate sharing of the heart that we also saw in the Old Testament passages. But Christlike friendship is framed not only with love, joy and intimacy, but also in terms of loyalty and self-sacrifice, giving to and supporting the other with everything that we have and whatever the cost. 'Greater love has no one than this: to lay down one's life for one's friends' (John 15:13 NIV).

Bible scholar Richard Bauckham makes a surprising connection between the biblical revelation of the glory of God and Jesus' love for his friends. 'It is in the thoroughly human love of Jesus for his friends that the divine love for the world takes human form.'[15] God's glory is revealed to its greatest extent in the self-sacrificial love that Jesus has for his *friends*.

Peter, James and John

It is clear from the Gospels that Jesus had developed a special closeness with Peter, James and John. They had been invited to accompany him on many of the most significant events, and supremely the three had been witnesses of the Transfiguration, when the glory of the Son of God was briefly revealed on earth.

> After six days Jesus took with him Peter, James and John the brother of James, and led them up a high mountain by themselves. There he was transfigured before them. His face shone like the sun, and his clothes became as white as the light. Just then there appeared before them Moses and Elijah, talking with Jesus.
> (Matthew 17:1–3 NIV)

Jesus chooses his most intimate friends to share this extraordinary revelation. He wishes those who are closest to him to be witnesses of his glory. And although Moses and Elijah have special symbolic relevance as representatives of the Old Testament Law and the Prophets respectively, I do wonder whether the description of the heavenly figures talking together can also be seen as a paradigm of heavenly friendship – these Old Testament heroes are experiencing an intimate sharing and openness with the transfigured Christ, just as Moses had experienced this face-to-face intimacy in his friendship with YHWH. So, the mount of the Transfiguration is not only a revelation of divine glory, it is also a revelation of divine–human intimacy – centred around the figure of the beloved Son.

The significance of the friendship of Peter, James and John is drawn out in the garden of Gethsemane. Matthew records that it was these three whom Jesus chose to be with him as he faced the awful prospect of the cross. I find it profoundly touching that he, the Son of God, asked his friends, weak, confused and exhausted as they were, to be with him at the time of his suffering. 'Stay here and keep watch' (Matthew 26:38). Even the Son of God did not want to face the prospect of death and the agony of the cross alone. He wanted his closest friends to be there, his heart-companions and loved ones.

Of the privileged three disciples, it is John who is celebrated as having the most wonderful and scandalous degree of closeness with Jesus. He is referred to repeatedly as 'the disciple who Jesus loved' using the Greek word *agape*.[16] As we saw earlier, in John 13:23, the literal Greek says that the beloved disciple was reclining in the bosom [*kolpos*] of Jesus, and John uses the same Greek word to describe the intimacy between the Father and the Son, 'the only God who is in the bosom [*kolpos*] of the Father, he has made him known' (John 1:18 literal translation). The twenty-first-century hermeneutic of suspicion inevitably causes some to wonder whether there was a homoerotic aspect to their relationship. Yet the intimacy of the friendship between Jesus and John was positively celebrated by the early Christian community and beyond.

Jesus had taught explicitly that sexual immorality [Greek *porneia*] was wrong, grouping it together with many other evils that came out of the human heart: 'For out of the heart come evil thoughts –

murder, adultery, sexual immorality [*porneia*], false witness, slander' (Matthew 15:19). Was it possible that Jesus did not regard a loving homoerotic relationship with another man as *porneia*?

I quote my friend Andrew Cornes:

> The Jews knew they were different from surrounding Greek and Roman cultures in two ways. They didn't worship idols. And sex was reserved for marriage. There's a general word in Greek for sex outside marriage: *porneia*. In Matthew and Mark, Jesus says this wells up from the human heart. For over seven years I've been researching a book on Greek and Roman homosexual relationships, including many that were loving, committed and generous. I believe I have studied every extant Jewish writing on the subject, between 200 BC and AD 200. They are absolutely univocal. They say that any homosexual sex is sin. So, when Jesus used the word translated as *porneia*, his hearers will have assumed that he included homosexual sex. If he did not regard that as sinful, he grossly misled his listeners.[17]

Among biblical commentators there does not appear to be a hint of suspicion about any sexual element in the intimacy between Jesus and the beloved disciple for twenty centuries, until the sexual obsessions of Freud and his followers started to cast a cloud of mistrust and paranoia.

But it is not just with the Twelve that Jesus develops deep and intimate friendships. The small family group of Mary, Martha and Lazarus in Bethany carries a special place in his heart. As has been well said, they were 'an ordinary family made extraordinary by Jesus'.[18] It is clear that the four loved to spend time together, sharing food and conversation. So, when Lazarus becomes critically unwell, Mary's urgent message is understandable: 'Lord, he whom you love [Greek *philio*] is ill' (John 11:3). Jesus is recorded as raising many people from the dead, but there is only one death in the Gospels in which Jesus is recorded as becoming so intensely and emotionally involved. He is 'deeply moved in his spirit', he is 'greatly troubled', he 'weeps'. Why this extraordinary emotional reaction? Of course, it is because of the intensity, warmth and intimacy of the friendships between them, and it is Mary's tears which break his heart. Even the onlookers are astonished at the extraordinary behaviour of the visiting rabbi, 'See how he loved him' (John 11:36).

Shortly after, following Lazarus' restoration to life, Mary, Martha and Lazarus have a joyful meal with Jesus, together with the other disciples (John 12:1–8). John emphasises that this incident happens only a matter of days before Jesus is to be crucified at the time of the Passover, the time that the sacrificial lamb was put to death. Mary, who had previously sat at Jesus' feet, now takes a litre of expensive perfume – a huge quantity equivalent to over 300 grams – stoops down to the feet of Jesus and anoints his feet with the precious ointment. Such is the quantity of the perfume that the whole house is filled with the fragrance. And then in a shocking and intimate act, she releases her hair, stoops down to his feet and tenderly wipes them with her hair. It is a strange and wonderful scene of extravagant sacrifice and intimate tenderness. Respectable Jewish women did not let down their hair in male company – this was something for the privacy of the bedroom.

Any orthodox rabbi would have instantly leapt back, in order to avoid the contamination of this woman's touch. But Jesus understands her heart and defends her from attack. He allows himself to be anointed in this tender and loving manner. His words are enigmatic, 'Leave her alone, she intended to keep it for the day of my burial' (v 7).

It may be that Mary had realised that Jesus' life was likely to end badly and she had secretly spent a huge amount of her savings in order to purchase the perfume so that Jesus' body could be anointed if the worse came to the worst. Jesus was aware of her loving intention. By this anointing, Mary was demonstrating her love for her closest friend, an act which encompasses humility and self-abasement, tenderness and extravagant willing sacrifice for the person of Christ.

It is interesting that this episode comes before John 13 when Jesus models sacrificial service by washing the feet of his disciples. Mary does not need to be taught about foot-washing, she does it instinctively and generously. Commentators have pointed out that because of the intensity and quantity of the perfume, the fragrance would still have been present when Jesus was crucified six days later. In other words, as Jesus hung on the cross he was smelling the fragrance of Mary's sacrificial act, the fragrance of sacrificial and costly love, the fragrance of friendship.

As we have seen, the biblical narrative sees disloyalty as representing the most painful rupture of deep covenant friendship. Seen through the prism of biblical friendship, the disloyalty and failures of Jesus' disciples at Gethsemane and Calvary hold a special resonance. Jesus had only recently bestowed the wonderful title of 'friends' on the group in the Upper Room but, despite this, 'all his disciples left him and fled' (Matthew 26:56).

Not all his friends behave in this way. It is the women who risk their lives by remaining at the cross as he dies. Mary Magdalene, Mary the mother of Jesus and Mary the mother of James and John, among others, are all recorded as being present. It is the women who watch where he is buried, who prepare spices over the Sabbath and who return to the tomb on Sunday morning. And the closeness and tenderness of the friendship between Jesus and Mary Magdalene are revealed in that poignant and evocative scene at the empty tomb:

> Jesus said to her 'Mary.' She turned and said to him in Aramaic, 'Rabboni!' (which means Teacher). Jesus said to her, 'Do not cling to me, for I have not yet ascended to the Father, but go to my brothers.'
> (John 20:16–17)

And after the shocking betrayal of Peter, his loyal friendship must be re-established in the three-fold questioning, 'Peter, do you love me?' In his repeated questioning in John 21, Jesus uses both Greek verbs for love, *agape* and *phileo*. Commentators have made much of the use of these two words, but perhaps the significance is that the deepest friendship with Jesus involves both elements. It is now recognised that the Greek words have overlapping meanings, although *agape* has the root meaning of self-giving and self-sacrifice for the other, while *phileo* tends to imply the joy and closeness of companionship. Loving Jesus involves both self-giving and joyful companionship, and Jesus is restoring Peter to both aspects of their friendship.[19]

Wonderfully, friendship with Jesus continues beyond Easter Sunday. The road to Emmaus provides a beautiful image of friends walking together. Just as the Creator came to the garden to walk with and to pass the time with his beloved friends, so the risen Son of God chooses to walk unrecognised with two of his friends, and to share supper with them. Although they were not part of the eleven, the two friends clearly knew Jesus well and had shared table fellowship with him on many occasions. The image of the unrecognised stranger who comes alongside to walk in companionship with us passes into Christian history as a precious paradigm of walking daily with Christ. 'Did not our hearts burn within us while he talked to us on the road, while he opened to us the Scriptures?' (Luke 24:32).

Carmen Caltagirone comments that, 'We too can have an Emmaus experience whenever we recognise Christ in a friend, an acquaintance, a colleague, our spouse or anyone who offers love.'[20]

Jesus loved to spend time sharing meals with his friends and after the resurrection he prepares a barbecue for them on a beach. Friendship with Jesus is part of the resurrection life and not even death on a cross can destroy the intimacy of this relationship. As Charles Spurgeon put it, 'In the heart of our Lord Jesus there burns such friendship towards us that all other forms of it are as dim candles to the sun'.[21]

Paul's network of friends in Romans 16

Theologian and friend Chris Wright has pointed out to me that the final chapter of Paul's magisterial letter to the Romans can be read as a very human commentary on the preceding fifteen chapters of profound theology. In particular, Romans 16 is a practical illustration of the preceding stress on unity in the gospel and the mutual acceptance of believers from both Jewish and Gentile backgrounds found in Romans 14 and 15. The final section of the book from Romans 15:23 onwards is a description of Paul's rich network of friends and co-workers who were linked with the Christian community in Rome:

> But now, since I no longer have any room for work in these regions, and since I have longed for many years to come to you, I hope to see you in passing as I go to Spain, and to be helped on my journey there by you, once I have enjoyed your company for a while.
> (Romans 15:23–24)

It's easy to hurry over these names in our Bible study, but it's helpful to pause for a moment and reflect on what this list in Romans 16 tells us about Paul's friendships. There is 'our sister Phoebe' who 'has been a patron [*prostatis* meaning benefactress] of many and of myself as well'. There are 'Prisca and Aquila, my fellow workers in Christ Jesus, who risked their necks for my life'. There is the beloved Epaenetus, Mary 'who has worked hard', Andronicus and Junia – kinsmen and fellow prisoners, Ampliatus – 'my beloved in the Lord', fellow worker Urbanus and the 'beloved Stachys'. And so the list goes on, including the mother of Rufus 'who has been a mother to me as well'.

In all, Paul greets twenty-six individuals by name, adding in most cases, as John Stott wrote in his commentary 'an appreciative personal reference'.[22] Prisca and Aquila were Jewish Christians, while many of the names were common names for slaves. Aristobolus, on the other hand is thought by many commentators to have been the grandson of Herod the Great and friend of the Emperor Claudius. John Stott also notes, 'The most interesting and instructive aspect . . . is that of gender. Nine out of the twenty-six persons greeted are women . . . Paul evidently thinks highly of them all.'

In this tantalisingly brief list of names we catch a glimpse of what it meant to Paul to live out the implications of the gospel which he proclaimed so powerfully. There is a rich and diverse network of sisters and brothers, mothers and fathers, from both Jewish and

Gentile backgrounds, elites and slaves. There is deep love, hard work, sacrificial care and practical support. And though not all of the friends have been greeted by name, they must all 'greet one another with a holy kiss' (v 16).

4

Gospel-crafted friendships

In subsequent chapters, I will describe something of the extraordinary breadth and depth of the friendships which John Stott developed with so many people around the world – friends, it seems, from virtually every social strata and every racial group. In many ways his friendships in the gospel seemed to represent a modern-day version of those of the Apostle Paul. I have struggled to find words to describe the essential characteristics of his friendships. But as I have already mentioned there is one phrase which has haunted and inspired me. It comes from a private conversation with David Zac Niringiye. As Zac movingly recounted the way that friendship with Stott had changed and influenced his life, I asked him what it was about his friendship that was so special. Zac paused. 'It was a friendship carved out of the heart of the gospel,' he said. It's a concept which has framed my reflections about friendship and I have tried to weave this idea into my writing. Gospel-crafted friendship. A deep and intimate bond formed, crafted and shaped by the transformative power of the gospel.

I have grown to see that there is a profound connection between the gospel and human friendship. The gospel, the good news about Jesus, concerns the re-creation and renewal of everything and everyone for communion, through the person of Christ. And the deepest and most intimate friendships between Christian believers can become a living embodiment, a tangible enactment, of the restoration of communion between broken human beings which the gospel enables.

In this chapter I try to lay out briefly what I see as the essential features of friendships that are shaped and crafted out of the heart of the gospel. They are friendships which are founded on what I like to think of as the *logic* of the gospel. They are energised by the power of the gospel, the good news about Jesus Christ. They are founded on the principles of the gospel, their goals are gospel goals, and as these friendships grow and deepen they should increasingly reflect the characteristics of the gospel.

I have briefly listed below twelve characteristics of gospel-crafted friendships. Of course, the list is not exclusive and you may wish to add to it or divide it up differently. Every deep and intimate friendship is unique because it is a bond between two unique individuals. Friendships are constantly changing because human beings and human love is never static. Nevertheless, it's possible to identify certain repeating themes that recur in all healthy and intimate friendships between Christian believers and it is these I have tried to draw out. As we will see, I think it is possible to identify all of these twelve characteristics, to a greater or lesser extent, in the deep friendships that John Stott developed and nurtured over his life, and in the deep covenantal friendships which ordinary believers in Christ have experienced over two thousand years of Christian history as they have tried to live and walk together in the light of the gospel.

Energised by the power of the gospel

1 Truthful, transparent and non-deceptive

Gospel-crafted friendships are truthful, transparent and non-deceptive. The gospel is founded on truth – and healthy friendship can only flourish in an atmosphere where there is truth, trust, honesty and authenticity. We are called to walk in the light with one another. And so it is immediately apparent that the deception and lies that lie at the heart of the historical abuse scandals represent a profound violation of the truth that healthy friendships must be built on. Genuine friendship can only flourish where there is truth and transparency on both sides, and whenever deception and concealment enter the relationship there is a risk of abuse and harm.

2 Committed to spiritual growth

They are based on a common commitment to spiritual growth and to encouraging Christlikeness and dependence on God. C. S. Lewis wrote that deep friendships are always 'about something'.[1] They are not aimless and directionless. There are shared enthusiasms, interests and goals. And so gospel-crafted friendships too are 'about something'. They are orientated towards the good of the other person, and in particular to spiritual growth in Christlikeness and fruitfulness, to the formation of the heart, and to the growth of God's kingdom. Just like the gospel, these friendships have an orientation – they point to the future in which we grow together to become more like Christ, looking for that ultimate fulfilment of our friendship, when together we will see him face-to-face.

3 Covenantal

The deepest and most significant friendships are covenantal, expressing either openly or implicitly a lifelong commitment of loyalty, mutual support, encouragement and love. Gospel-crafted friendships reflect the covenant 'steadfast love' of God's heart, expressed, as we have already seen, in the rich Hebrew word *chesed*. The God revealed in the Scriptures is abounding, overflowing in covenant love. Not all our friendships and relationships can bear the weight of this kind of commitment. But our deepest and most intimate friendships are called to reflect God's deepest heart, overflowing with *chesed*. These friendships call us to a voluntary, and frequently lifelong, commitment to seek the good of the other. A wonderful theme of biblical friendships is that our true friends are loyal and they will be with us when adversity strikes. And this is what our deepest friends promise – to 'be there', whatever it costs, until 'death do us part'.

4 Sharing and respectful

They are mutually sharing and respectful. There is no hierarchy in gospel-crafted friendships, because we are all equally needy before the gospel. Although one friend may have much greater knowledge, wisdom and life experience than the other, we are both pilgrims on the Way, and we are helping and learning from one another as we journey along. As we have seen, the image of 'walking together' is a profound biblical symbol of friendship. Gospel-crafted friendships reveal a deep equality and mutuality, rather than a hierarchical and 'one-way' relationship which may be more appropriate between a mentor and a client, or a pastor and a needy soul. In our friendships with John Stott, many young people, including myself, found a surprising sense of mutuality. In spite of our youth and inexperience, he was capable of respecting us, sharing his heart with us, and willing and open to learn from us.

5 Vulnerable, humble and servant-hearted

They enable us to be vulnerable and broken with one another; they are based on humility, servant-heartedness and self-sacrifice. The gospel of Jesus reveals us to ourselves as broken sinners and then points to the source of boundless forgiveness. Building on the forgiveness of the gospel, our friendships therefore enable each of us to be vulnerable with the other, to share our brokenness and, where necessary, to ask for forgiveness. Gospel-crafted friendships are founded on the endless grace of God.

Henri Nouwen wrote:

When we honestly ask ourselves which persons in our lives mean the most to us, we often find that it is those who, instead of giving much advice, solutions, or cures, have chosen rather to share our pain and touch our wounds with a gentle and tender hand. The friend who can be silent with us in a moment of despair or confusion, who can stay with us in an hour of grief and bereavement, who can tolerate not-knowing, not-curing, not-healing, and face with us the reality of our powerlessness, that is the friend who cares.[2]

Carmen Caltagirone writes:

We enter into intimacy with those we dare to reveal our deepest thoughts ... With our soulmates we share the experience of

63

knowing and being known. Heart speaks to heart and two are bonded together and become one.[3]

In friendship our goal is to serve the other. We do not stand on our rights but follow Christ as he models sacrificial servant leadership, the washing of feet. Gospel-crafted friendships are based on *kenosis*, the self-emptying of Christ, which is at the heart of the gospel.

6 Crossing barriers

They overcome all social barriers – age, class, social status, gender and race. This is one of the striking characteristics of many gospel-shaped friendships. It is most natural for us to have the closest friendships with those who are most similar to us – in age, social status, racial origins and so on. This, after all, was Aristotle's vision of perfect friendship. But the unexpected gift of the gospel is that it is possible to find deep bonds of unity in Christ with those who are completely different from us. Gospel-shaped friendships frequently cross barriers of age, status, racial origins, background and abilities. Some of the most profound and meaningful bonds develop between so-called 'healthy' people and those with disabilities, learning difficulties and mental health problems. Gospel-shaped friendships can teach us to look beyond the surface to see the hidden heart of the other.

In his final book, Henri Nouwen wrote movingly of his friendship with Adam, a profoundly disabled young man.

Adam's humanity was not diminished by his disabilities. Adam's humanity was a full humanity, in which the fullness of love became visible for me, and for others who grew to know him. Yes, I began to love Adam with a love that transcended most of the feelings, emotions, and passions that I had associated with love among people. Adam couldn't say, 'I love you,' he couldn't embrace me spontaneously or express gratitude in words. Still I dare to say we loved each other with a love that was as enfleshed as any love, and was at the same time truly spiritual. We were friends, brothers, bonded in our hearts.[4]

As we overcome the barriers between us, we discover a deeper unity. And, paradoxically, it is by exploring and revelling in our differences that we so often discover the fun, the spark, the humour and the special joy of our friendship.

7 Prayerful

They are prayerful – because the work of the gospel is a spiritual work and can only be done through prayer and dependence on God. Matthew Smith, one of John Stott's last study assistants, described to me how when John Stott was in London he would spend an hour or so every day writing and dictating personal letters to his friends. His memory for details was phenomenal. He remembered the names of children, spouses and close relatives, dates and events. And his memory for details was based on his regular and disciplined prayer for each individual that he knew and loved. Stott's friendships were bathed in prayer. When asked at the end of his life, what he would have done differently if he could live his life again, Stott answered, 'I would have prayed more.'[5]

Friendships with boundaries

So far we have looked at seven positive characteristics of healthy, gospel-crafted friendships. But following the recent scandals that have beset the church, we cannot avoid the recognition that what appeared outwardly to be close friendships have led to lasting damage. In order to build deep and intimate friendships that reflect the values of the gospel, we need to understand and follow the rules and boundaries which are necessary to ensure that friendships are safe, healthy and transparent.

Jim Packer, in his influential book *Knowing God*, argued that having God's wisdom did not mean having a divine perspective on every aspect of the world. Instead, he used a helpful analogy for living with divine wisdom.

... it is like being taught to drive. What matters in driving is the speed and appropriateness of your reactions to things ... You do not ask why the road should narrow or screw itself into a dog-leg, nor why that van should be parked where it is ... you simply try to see and do the right thing in the actual situation that presents itself. The effect of divine wisdom is to enable you and me to do just that in the actual situation of everyday life. To drive well you have to keep your eyes skinned to notice exactly what is in front of you. To live wisely, you have to be clear-sighted and realistic – ruthlessly so – in looking at life as it is.[6]

As I have reflected on this analogy, I have seen how helpful it is. Living in a wise and godly way, just like skilled driving, is a process of continual improvisation in the perpetually changing contingencies and choices which daily life presents. Every skilled driver needs to know and understand what the rules and boundaries of safe driving are. An expert driver is both free and, at the same time, makes sure to follow the rules. They are free to choose whether to overtake now, or to hold back, but throughout the journey they understand and follow the rules for safe overtaking. In order to drive safely they need to be completely realistic about the risks that driving involves, but this realism and wisdom allows freedom to enjoy their journey with safety and security.

In the same way we need to understand and follow the rules and boundaries of safe friendships. As Jim Packer wrote, 'To live wisely, you have to be clear-sighted and realistic – ruthlessly so – in looking at life as it is.' And this is nowhere more true than in our closest and most intimate relationships.

The next three criteria for healthy gospel-crafted friendships are of special importance because they represent the three boundaries that seem to me to be essential to protect the integrity of these relationships. These are the rules of the road for safe driving. When these boundaries are ignored out of carelessness or intentionally breached for predatory and selfish reasons, there is a risk of tragic and permanent harm resulting. The historic abuse scandals of the last twenty years have repeatedly demonstrated the lifelong harm that can result, especially to those who are most vulnerable. The three boundaries, which we will return to discuss in greater detail in a later chapter, are:

- non-sexual
- non-abusive, non-coercive and non-manipulative
- non-exclusive.

Let's look at each of these in a little more detail.

8 Non-sexual

Gospel-crafted friendships must be sharply differentiated from sexual relationships. The gospel values, honours and protects sexual purity and the sanctity of the exclusive marital bond. So, in orthodox biblical thinking, all physical sexual expression should be confined exclusively to heterosexual marriage, which is intended to be monogamous and lifelong. In contrast, gospel-shaped friendships are based on deep, intimate love – but it is a non-sexual love. Of course, we are sexual beings and all our relationships are in some sense influenced by our own gender and sexual nature. However, if any form of sexual intimacy, erotic fantasy or sexual gratification enter a friendship, the nature of that relationship is at risk of becoming irrevocably changed and distorted. We start to use the other as a means to our own sexual gratification.

Contemporary culture repeatedly blurs the distinction between close friendship and sexually expressed intimacy. But it seems to me that Christian thinking from biblical times onwards has always maintained a sharp and clear distinction between the two. However, it is important to emphasise that maintaining the non-sexual boundary does not mean that there must be no physical expression of friendship. When it seems appropriate and welcomed, a warm hug, an arm round the shoulder, holding hands and so on can be a precious way in which close friendship can be expressed and cemented. Many single, celibate people in our churches feel that they are deprived of hugs and warm physical contact because in a hypersexualised society we have become so cautious and suspicious about touch. This is a theme we will return to in a later chapter.

9 Non-abusive, non-coercive and non-manipulative

Gospel-shaped friendships are respectful, non-coercive and non-manipulative. As we saw previously, the hermeneutic of suspicion perceives a covert drive to power, to dominate and master another, as the energising force behind many deep relationships. But the gospel approach to power is never coercive. Instead, we see in Jesus a revolutionary attitude to power, based on voluntary emptying and restraint in order to serve and love the other.

> In your relationships with one another, have the same mindset as Christ Jesus:
>
> who being in very nature God,
>   did not consider equality with God something
>   to be used to his own advantage;
> rather he made himself nothing
>   by taking the very nature of a servant,
>   being made in human likeness.
> And being found in appearance as a man
>   he humbled himself
>   by becoming obedient to death –
>   even death on a cross.
> (Philippians 2:5–8 NIV)

The keynote attitude in gospel-crafted friendships is one of respect for the other. Respect for the weaker member in a friendship, as a wonderful and unique person made in God's image. All forms of covert coercion, control and manipulation are incompatible with genuine respect, and part of this respect means allowing people to have room to disagree with us, to grow and explore their own views and perspectives.

As Henri Nouwen points out, respect for the other leads to a willingness to offer them space, to avoid the risk of becoming manipulative, oppressive and smothering in our demands.

> Friendship requires a constant willingness to forgive each other for not being Christ and a willingness to ask Christ himself to be the true centre. When Christ does not mediate a relationship, that relationship easily becomes demanding, manipulating, oppressive, an arena for many forms of rejection. An unmediated friendship cannot last long; you simply expect too much of the other and cannot offer the other the space he or she needs to grow.[7]

Gospel-shaped friendships thrive on genuine and uncoerced freedom. That means that instead of clinging on for selfish motives, we must offer the other person the freedom to disagree violently with us and even walk away from us, though it may cause us deep pain and a sense of rejection. We may ask for forgiveness and reconciliation but, in the end, respect means we allow the other to walk away.

10 Non-exclusive

Gospel-crafted friendships are generous to others and non-exclusive. In striking contrast to the union of marriage, which is safeguarded by a barrier of faithfulness and exclusivity, gospel-shaped friendships are, by their very nature, non-exclusive. As we all know, in marriage, any hint of unfaithfulness strikes at the heart of the relationship. When the barrier of exclusivity is breached, the marriage is damaged and at risk of permanent destruction. In contrast, gospel-shaped friendships do not exclude and separate out from others. They are not weakened when new friendships are developed. Healthy friendships positively encourage and delight in welcoming others and extending bonds with new people.

Any attempt to 'grab-on' to the other, to bind them to oneself to the exclusion of others, has the effect of distorting and weaponising the relationship, leading to a real risk of harm and ultimate breakdown. We cannot fulfil all our God-given needs for intimacy and companionship in a single individual and if we attempt to do so, we will damage and distort the relationship. Instead, we are created to flourish within a non-exclusive network of close and intimate friendships.

Friendships that point to Christ

Finally, we turn to the heart of gospel-crafted friendship – the wonderful future that they point to and the one who makes them possible.

11 Filled with faith, hope and love

Gospel-crafted friendships are filled with faith, hope and love. These three New Testament qualities are often described as 'eschatological virtues' because, while they are life-giving realities for our Christian walk here on earth, they also point to the consummation of history and to the new heaven and new earth. Ultimately, the real meaning and value of our gospel-crafted friendships, these costly, time-consuming and wonderful relationships, will only be seen in the world to come. Friendships are a hidden ministry of faith, hope and love. Just as these three will endure into the new creation, so it seems will our friendships. In fact, our deepest friendships are a foretaste of what is to come.[8] As we enter into, nurture and develop gospel-crafted friendships, we do not know what the future will hold. There may be loss, pain and temporary separation to come. But we know that this is not the end of the story.

Henri Nouwen wrote:

True friendships are lasting because true love is eternal. A friendship in which heart speaks to heart is a gift from God, and no gift that comes from God is temporary or occasional. All that comes from God participates in God's eternal life. Love between people, when given by God, is stronger than death. In this sense, true friendships continue beyond the boundary of death. When you have loved deeply that love can grow even stronger after the death of the person you love . . . You have to trust that every true friendship has no end, that a communion of saints exists among all those, living and dead, who have truly loved God and one another. You know from experience how real this is. Those you have loved deeply and who have died live on in you, not just as memories but as real presences.[9]

12 Christ-centred

Above all, gospel-shaped friendships are Christ-centred. Gospel-shaped friendships are centred on Christ and are mediated by Christ, as he himself promised, 'Where two or three are gathered in my name, there am I in the midst' (Matthew 18:20 KJV). As our friendship grows and deepens, we are coming closer to Christ. I am being drawn to Christ in the other person and they are being drawn to Christ in me. As Dietrich Bonhoeffer put it, 'The more genuine and the deeper our community becomes, the more will everything else between us recede, the more clearly and purely will Jesus Christ and his work become the one and only thing that is vital between us.'[10]

In the next two chapters as we turn to look at John Stott's practice of friendships, I think it is helpful to keep this theoretical framework in mind. How were the features of gospel-crafted friendships expressed in his own life and relationships? What can we learn about the nurturing of healthy Christian friendships from John Stott, and how can we translate his vision and personal practice into realistic action in our own time?

But, at the same time as we look back from the vantage of the 2020s, we cannot ignore the all-pervasive hermeneutic of suspicion. The painful truth is that sometimes suspicion is warranted. As we will discuss in greater detail in a later chapter, there has been a sad litany of charming, gifted and persuasive Christian leaders who have turned out to be involved in abusive relationships with younger people who were under their influence.

By contrast, what can we learn about the nurturing of *healthy* Christian friendships from John Stott? What steps did he take to avoid the possibility of coercion and abuse of those who were vulnerable? And how can we translate his vision and personal practice into realistic action in our own time?

5

Would you like to have a cup of coffee with me?

The story of John Stott's early life has been told many times. The elite background with a Harley Street consultant father, Arnold Stott. Education at the elite fee-paying Rugby School where, as a seventeen-year-old, he attended a meeting at which the visiting clergyman Eric Nash, universally known as 'Bash', spoke about the challenging figure of Jesus. That night Stott prayed alone in his dormitory 'opening the door' to Christ. John Stott wrote to Bash, telling him what he had done, and in response Bash began a regular correspondence of letters.

Here are Stott's own words:

> . . . he must have written to me once a week for at least five years. I still marvel at his faithfulness. For often they were long letters, broken into paragraphs with sectional headings underlined. Some paragraphs were heavily theological . . . others were ethical . . . There was personal counsel too, especially on the need to get ten hours' sleep every night. Then every letter would end with a 'best thought', some precious biblical text opened and applied. Alongside the best thought however, often as a postscript and perhaps always a deliberate prophylactic against an excess of piety, he would add a joke, usually of the schoolboy howler variety.[1]

The Second World War broke out soon after Stott's conversion and he later wrote:

> I was a very immature Christian, barely eighteen months old and would describe myself as an instinctive pacifist. I had now

read the Sermon on the Mount for the first time with its commands not to resist evil but rather to turn the other cheek and to love our enemies. It seemed to me impossible to reconcile these injunctions with war. Nobody introduced me to the just war theory or helped me to balance the biblical arguments.[2]

Stott's decision to become a Conscientious Objector led to an extremely painful break with his father who was a Major-General in the Army Medical Service.

For about two years he found it virtually impossible to speak to me, and could not make up his mind whether he could continue to support me at Cambridge University ... It was because of this alienation from my father that Bash became almost a surrogate father to me. He was very sympathetic towards me in my dilemma. At the same time he was never weak or sentimental. He could easily be disappointed. His letters to me often contained rebuke, for I was a wayward young Christian and needed to be disciplined. In fact so frequent were his admonitions at one period that, whenever I saw his familiar writing on an envelope, I needed to pray and prepare myself for half an hour before I felt ready to open it.[3]

Stott's description of 'a surrogate father', might be seen, through the hermeneutic of suspicion, as an unhealthy emotional dependence and attraction of a lonely student for a much older single man. But there is an important gospel point here, which John Stott frequently expounded from the New Testament. For many whose biological family relationships are broken and alienated, the Christian community of faith provides *a new family*. We are brought into a new community, founded on the gospel, in which we discover that we have fathers and mothers, sisters and brothers, aunts and uncles, and so on. It is a New Testament theme which Stott was delighted to draw out on many occasions in his preaching and writing.

It was Jesus himself who, pointing to his disciples, said, 'Here are my mother and my brothers! For whoever does the will of my Father in heaven is my brother and sister and mother' (Matthew 12:49–50). And Paul instructed Timothy to treat an older man in the local church community 'as if he were your father. Treat younger men as brothers, older women as mothers, and younger women as sisters, with absolute purity' (1 Timothy 5:1–2 NIV).

I know from private conversations with John Stott how much the warmth and love he received from Christian family members across the world meant to him, throughout his life – particularly given the painful alienation he had experienced with his own biological family, and the loneliness that his single life could entail.

During his time as an undergraduate and then ordinand at Cambridge University, the wartime years of 1940–5, John Stott played a key part as leader at numerous Christian holiday camps run by Bash, for privileged, fee-paying 'public school' boys. In fact, Bash wrote a letter in 1941 stating formally that if 'anything should happen to me', he wished John Stott to 'assume full and absolute control' of the ministry that he had started.[4] There is no doubt that Bash's model of deeply committed, prayerful, loyal friendship was extraordinarily influential for the younger Stott.

It might have seemed inevitable, coming from such a restricted and entitled background, that Stott would be destined to inhabit the comfortable prejudices and blind spots of the English upper classes. But from the time of John Stott's ordination and his starting work as a curate at All Souls Church, Langham Place, London in December 1945, it seems clear that he quietly but firmly distinguished his ministry and efforts from that of the socially elite 'Bash camps'.

The parish of All Souls, in post-war inner London, contained areas of extraordinary poverty and deprivation, with bombed-out buildings and numerous homeless individuals. Stott became deeply concerned about how to reach out to those with the deepest needs, even spending a couple of nights as a homeless vagrant on the Thames Embankment in order to experience what it meant to be part of London's underclass.[5]

Shortly after becoming a curate at All Souls, John Stott started organising summer camps for boys. But instead of inviting the elite 'public school' boys, Stott invited a group of young lads from the parish and the adjacent Soho district of London. It was, in retrospect, the social mirror-image of the 'Bash camps'. Although Stott remained unfailingly loyal to Nash himself, it is clear that from 1945 onwards he was quietly following a very different trajectory.

Although he had the wonderful gift of being able to relate naturally and unselfconsciously with people from all social backgrounds, he was always drawn to and fascinated by those who were different – especially those who didn't count socially, those who were at risk of being ignored. On innumerable occasions I watched him in a restaurant, cafeteria or conference dining room, reaching out in simple friendship to those who were serving behind the counters, while the rest of us were concentrating on choosing and devouring our food!

Would you like to have a cup of coffee with me?

In October 1972, I moved to London to start medical studies at St Thomas's Hospital Medical School, part of the University of London. I started regularly attending All Souls Church shortly afterwards, drawn (I must admit) not by the calibre of the biblical preaching, but by the newly formed church orchestra, founded by Noel Tredinnick. Here was an opportunity to exercise my modest skills as an amateur trumpet player. I also joined the choir and I remember an occasional snatched word with John Stott as we waited, robed, in the vestry before processing into the chancel.

My memories of that period were that Stott appeared a rather austere and slightly intimidating figure in the pulpit. However, I was immediately captivated by the spiritual depth, intellectual content and the extraordinary detail that he packed into his sermons. I found myself furiously making notes during the sermons, trying to capture as much as possible. It was like drinking from a fire hose.

I can still remember an early series of sermons on 'Issues Facing Christians Today'. This was the 1970s and the sermons were on topics like labour relations, nuclear disarmament, divorce law reform and so on. I had never heard sermons like this. Stott was taking verbatim quotes from the newspapers and commentators of that time and carefully and persuasively showing how Christian truth could engage directly, demonstrating the relevance and the power of Christian thinking. I can still recall the impact those sermons had on me and his example of careful, respectful and thoughtful engagement with secular thinkers and commentators has remained a role model over the succeeding decades.

Later on, in 1974, as a second-year medical student, to my utter astonishment, I receive a message from the Rectory. 'Would you like to come and have a cup of coffee with me?' My first reaction was one of alarm; it was like being asked to see the headmaster in his study. Have I been found guilty of some deep doctrinal error or misdeed? I still remember that mixture of apprehension and anticipation as I walk down the quiet cobbled mews and approach the door at the appointed time.

He welcomes me in person and I ascend the spiral staircase to his tiny bachelor flat, just two rooms and a kitchenette, where he solemnly prepares a cup of instant coffee for me and offers a chocolate digestive biscuit. In truth I cannot remember much of that first private conversation, but I do remember the sense of astonishment and wonder that this outstanding and venerated Christian leader wished to spend time with me. I was immediately aware of gentle, courteous but penetrating questioning. He seemed genuinely interested in me as a person, in my background and family, my Christian journey, my musical interests, my involvement in London University Christian Union, my thoughts and opinions.

I do remember, at that very first meeting, a deep intuitive sense of his Christlike authenticity and humility. Over the years I have had the privilege of meeting a number of prominent Christian speakers and preachers. I have listened to them in the pulpit with awe and admiration at their eloquence, persuasive abilities, charm and apparent spirituality. But then, on several occasions, meeting the same person in private, I have had a sense of disappointment. They were impressive in public but less so in private. They seemed diminished once they were out of the spotlight. There was a sense that they had adopted a *persona* in the pulpit that was not entirely authentic.

But alone with John Stott, I had the opposite sensation. Yes, he was impressive, charming and authoritative in the pulpit, but in truth he was far more impressive in private – sharing his heart, his deepest concerns, his personal prayers, with nobody watching. As you got to know him, it became apparent that he wasn't putting on an act. Instead, he was completely committed to living out every day what he preached from the pulpit, as a humble and authentic follower of Christ. He made you hungry for an undefinable quality of his life and character. As I got to know him, it became obvious that he lived and prayed in the way he preached. His authenticity, his humility and his concern, interest and love for ordinary people, the people 'who didn't count', left an indelible impact.

There was no sense that I was being recruited into a pre-arranged programme or training syllabus. There was no obvious agenda or goal to our conversation. He didn't offer to give me a series of weekly Bible studies. Instead, to my utter astonishment, it seemed that he was gently and courteously offering himself. As I walked away down the mews an hour or so later, I found it hard to take in what had just happened. But I do remember praying something like, 'Lord, I know I can't be like him, but please, please, just give me a touch of what he has.' It was a silent prayer I was to repeat on many occasions as I left his presence.

And so started a friendship which lasted for more than thirty years. He became a spiritual father to me as he was to so many others. We walked together, sharing our lives and hearts through triumphs, tragedies and health crises from 1974 until his death in 2011. And his friendship, vision, example and gentle godly influence were to become defining factors in my life, changing the direction of my career, my priorities and my preoccupations.

Although I had no awareness of this at the time, it is now well known that in the early 1970s, John Stott was on his own spiritual and intellectual journey. The story of his life and ministry has been recounted in great detail elsewhere and I will only sketch out a few of the details as they impacted our friendship.[6] His early ministry in the 1940s and 1950s as an evangelist and Bible teacher, particularly among university students, had been extremely fruitful. But in the late 1960s there was a growing awareness that the tectonic plates of Western society were shifting. Sexual liberation and 'free love', student protests and anarchic anti-authoritarianism were rampant. Scientific advances were transforming the world and the first humans had landed on the moon. Sweeping legal reforms were changing attitudes to abortion, homosexuality, divorce and race relations.

I remember Stott recounting a particular incident which had clearly deeply troubled him. He was talking to a couple of students who had been brought up in Christian homes but who were now repudiating the faith of their parents.

'So,' I said to them, 'tell me about it, what has happened to you. Is it that you no longer believe that Christianity is true?'

'No,' they said, 'that's not our problem and if you could persuade us that Christianity is true, I'm not so sure that we would accept it.'

'Then what is your problem?' I asked with some surprise.

'Our problem,' they replied, 'is not whether Christianity is true, but whether it is relevant. And frankly we do not see how it can be. For Christianity arose in a primitive Palestinian culture. What has an ancient Palestinian religion to do with us who live in the exciting, kaleidoscopic world of the end of the twentieth century? We had men on the moon in the 1970s and we will have men on Mars in the 1980s. We have transplant surgery today and genetic engineering tomorrow. What has your primitive religion to say to us?'[7]

From many similar encounters, John Stott became increasingly convinced that, although it remained vital to defend the truthfulness of historic biblical Christianity, it was equally important to demonstrate the *relevance* of Christian truth to the real-world, contemporary issues and problems with which many students, intellectuals, thinkers and ordinary people were preoccupied. It was not enough to faithfully *proclaim* the truth as we had been taught it, if we are to be authentic disciples of Christ, we must learn to *listen* and *understand* the modern world in which we have been placed as witnesses.[8]

The emphasis on listening was a constant refrain in Stott's teaching and I was repeatedly struck by his commitment to put it into practice. Listening to God, listening to the world, listening to fellow Christians in the global Christian community. His commitment to listening to others was grounded in an attitude of *respect*. It was that note of genuine respect that one sensed when talking to him – a quality of respect which undergirded the desire to genuinely listen and not just to pretend.

Respect for God and his Word, certainly. Stott often talked about humbling ourselves before God's truth and allowing it to exercise authority over our thinking and behaviour. But also respect for the other, especially for those who were different and for those who oppose us and all that we stand for. Respect for their humanity, for their creation in God's image, for their life experience, for their suffering, for their intellectual integrity and for the grace of God in their lives. Stott believed firmly in the Reformation concept of common grace – that God gave good things to the righteous and the unrighteous. So, respect for the other leads naturally to careful listening, and a desire to understand, rather than to bludgeon others with our opinions and beliefs.

Stott's commitment to listening to the modern world led him to start a reading group for young people and shortly after our first meeting in 1974, he invited me to become a member of this group, comprising maybe a dozen of Stott's younger friends. We met monthly or so when he was in London, agreeing in advance to read a book that seemed influential and significant within the contemporary culture. We used to meet in Stott's study and the discussion flowed freely between us, with only an occasional intervention or question from Stott himself. He encouraged us both to try to fully engage with and understand the mind and intentions of the author, but then to debate how we should respond to the author from the perspective of the Christian faith. We read many cult modern novels of the 1970s, *Zen and the Art of Motorcycle Maintenance* by Robert Pirsig, the novels of Hermann Hesse, Carlos Castaneda, Franz Kafka and John Fowles. A number of times we composed and sent a joint letter to the author, via the publishers, even receiving replies on two or three occasions.

As time went by, we became more adventurous, branching out into popular science (Richard Dawkins and Arthur C. Clarke), films (Ingmar Bergman, Steven Spielberg, Woody Allen), arthouse plays (*Whose Life Is It Anyway?*, *Duet for One*), even *Cosmopolitan* magazine. Over the years I became more aware of the extraordinary privilege of taking part in this group. The sense of exploring and engaging together in the strange and wonderful cultural world we found ourselves in, learning from one another under Stott's benign and perceptive chairmanship, a sense of optimism and excitement as we discovered new riches in the relevance and power of biblical Christian teaching applied to our culture. As we met month by month, our mutual friendship, enjoyment and openness with one another grew. Those evenings in Stott's study in Bridford Mews remain imprinted on my mind, becoming some of the most formative and transformative experiences of my life.

My good friend Vinoth Ramachandra wrote about an influential experience in the same reading group.

Although I heard John Stott as a speaker and read some of his books during my undergraduate years in London, it was only in the final year of my postgraduate study that I got to know him personally, when he invited me to join the reading group that met quarterly in his flat. One of my vivid memories of that group was going to watch a film (the title eludes me) by the renowned Swedish existentialist Ingmar Bergman. Stott was so deeply moved by the film that he insisted on taking us all to a nearby church where he knelt before the Lord's Table and poured out his soul in contrition over all his flawed relationships. It is such integrity and vulnerability that leave an indelible impression on young people's minds. And it is the memory of Stott's character, far more than his books or preaching, that

I recall whenever I grow discouraged by the hypocrisies or arrogance of so many in leadership positions today.[9]

There's no doubt that John Stott too found the reading group stimulating and valuable. He devoted several pages to the group in his book *I Believe in Preaching*, published in 1982, describing it in characteristically Stottian prose:

> What kind of study, then will increase our understanding of the modern world? I want to bear witness to the immense stimulus which I have myself received from the reading group which I helped to bring into being in 1974 . . . We have tried to concentrate on secular rather than religious books, because the main purpose of our group is to help us understand the secular mind of the post-Christian West, in order to combat it with a Christian mind. I have tried therefore to encourage the group to take responsibility for each month's choice and they have certainly selected some titles which I would otherwise never have heard of . . . The experience of the reading group – of the books we have read, the films and plays we have seen, and the discussion they have provoked – has not only increased our understanding of the modern world, but excited our compassion for human beings in their lostness and despair, confirmed our Christian faith and rekindled our sense of Christian mission . . . The London group has given me the necessary stimulus to read at least some of the books I ought to be reading and has provided me with some sharp-witted, warm-hearted young people as a congenial context in which to discuss the issues raised. They have helped to drag me into the modern world and have planted my feet on the soil of contemporary reality: I am very grateful to them.[10]

I think it was at one of the reading group meetings that the term 'Uncle John' was first used. At the end of the meeting the discussion had turned for some reason to how we should address him. 'Mr Stott' or 'Rector' seemed impersonal, 'John' seemed impertinent. Someone suggested 'Uncle John', since he had always emphasised the importance of discovering our new identities within the Christian church family. Stott clearly approved of this epithet and it stuck, right to the end of his life. Years later, I do remember him quietly informing me that as I was now a Professor and a senior member of the medical profession, it would be entirely appropriate for me to call him 'John', but he remained Uncle John to me and to most of us to the end.

On reflection it is obvious that John Stott always viewed everyday social events as a means of initiating, strengthening, investing in and renewing friendships. Although his disciplined daily routine of prayer, Bible study, sermon preparation, correspondence and writing involved long hours of solitary concentration, it seemed that when he was not actively working or studying he did not particularly enjoy solitude. He did not have a predilection for solitary walks or for spending time alone. Instead, he seemed intensely social and gregarious. Every meal was an opportunity to get to know someone else better. Every visit to Hampstead Heath or Regent's Park, every birdwatching trip, every visit to a new city – none of these were of any interest unless they were in the company of friends.

And it gradually became apparent that, just as he was thoughtful, prayerful and intentional about everything he did, so he was very intentional about whom he invited to join him at each event. Seen through the all-pervasive hermeneutic of suspicion, it would be easy to regard Stott's practice of intentional friendship as manipulative, elitist, even predatory. Was it a classic example of a powerful and privileged man creating an inner circle of privileged, elitist younger men who were groomed and indoctrinated for future leadership?

Of course, there is always a risk that close friendship between a small group becomes introverted and exclusive, leading to the creation of an Inner Ring, as famously described by C. S. Lewis:

> I believe that in all men's lives at certain periods, and in many men's lives at all periods between infancy and extreme old age, one of the most dominant elements is the desire to be inside the local Ring and the terror of being left outside.[11]

But, in reality, Stott delighted in developing and investing in friendships with an extraordinary range of men and women, young and old, across a wide range of social and educational backgrounds. He modelled a practice of generous, outgoing and non-exclusive friendship that was extraordinarily positive and life-enhancing. Very many of his friends came from 'majority world' backgrounds, whom he had met and befriended on his frequent international travels. And I am struck by how few of his younger friends came from the privileged and socially elite class of his own background.

Although he always expressed gratitude for Bash and for his prayerful and fatherly care for him as a young Christian, Stott's own practice of friendship seemed rather different. He frequently wrote personal letters to his friends around the world, but they were rarely, if ever, critical, rebuking or disciplinary. Whereas Stott could write of Bash that, 'He could easily be disappointed. His letters to me often contained rebuke, for I was a wayward young Christian and needed to be disciplined', the contrast with Stott's own letters could not be more marked.[12] His letters to me were unfailingly positive and encouraging. Whenever I saw his spindly handwriting on the envelope of a personal letter addressed to me, there was only anticipation, not trepidation. In the place of rebuke, Stott would sometimes ask penetrating and insightful questions, questions that were intended to illuminate mixed motives or confused thinking, questions that invited honest responses without insisting or coercing. As Rico Tice put it, as a son of a cardiologist, Stott had his father's diagnostic acumen.

The only rebuke I remember receiving was that I had not been to see him for many weeks. 'I'm very sorry that it's been so long since I was last visited.' He looked at me severely, 'Are you genuinely repentant?' 'Yes, I am, Uncle John. I'm sorry that it's been so long.' 'Then I must forgive you.'

Engaging in the world

As the years passed, it was Stott's understanding of 'incarnational mission' that became particularly significant for me. He frequently referred to the Great Commission in John's Gospel, 'Just as the Father has sent me, so also I am sending you' (John 20:21), explaining how the incarnation of Christ is both the model and the motivation for our engagement in the secular world. This transformed my view of my medical and scientific calling, and of the need to be salt and light in a corrupt and dark society. Stott crystallised his thoughts in *The Contemporary Christian*:

> . . . our mission is to be modelled on his. Indeed, all authentic mission is incarnational mission. It demands identification without loss of identity. It means entering other people's worlds, as he entered ours, though without compromising our Christian convictions, values or standards.[13]

Perhaps the first lesson I learnt from him about being a witness for Christ in a hostile secular world was that it's not about how clever our arguments are, or the brilliance of our apologetics or political strategy. Witness has to start with personal *authenticity, honesty and humility*. It matters much more who we are as people than what we actually say. In particular, it matters how we treat those who oppose us. Respect for other people is central, especially for those who oppose us and all that we stand for.

Stott also modelled the importance of *dialogue* with those with whom we disagree – 'a conversation in which each party is serious in their approach both to the subject and to the other person, and desires to listen and learn as well as to speak and instruct.'[14] He argued that true dialogue was a mark of authenticity. In dialogue, we share our common humanity and we express humility. As we listen carefully to the other, our respect for that person as a human being made in God's image grows. We realise we cannot sweep away all their convictions with a brash, unfeeling dismissal. We have to recognise that some of their misconceptions about Christianity may be our fault – and that because of us they are rejecting a caricature of the truth. As we listen to the other, we may have uncomfortable lessons to learn. We may have to repent of a lingering sense of our superiority. Our desire becomes not to score points or to humiliate the other, but to enter into their experience. Dialogue was also a mark of integrity. As we listen to the other, we listen to their real beliefs, problems and experiences, and we divest our minds of the false images we may have harboured.

Our goal is that out of our dialogue, our respectful engagement, the truth should emerge. But, argued Stott:

> . . . as a Christian I know that Christ is the truth and so I long for Christ himself to emerge. But since Christ makes demands on all, I may well find that my own understanding and commitment are revealed to be inadequate. So the dialogue will be challenging to myself as well as to the other person . . . It is a matter of personal integrity that I respect the freedom and dignity of the other person, of my dialogue partner, and I do not expect of him or her anything that I am not willing to ask or hope for myself.[15]

I had the opportunity of observing Stott as he modelled respectful dialogue in many different contexts, both with Christians of many different traditions and with those from an entirely secular background. I saw how he expended so much effort in trying to understand, asking thoughtful questions, requesting clarification. This was not just an opportunity for him to go on about his own preoccupations – he wanted to listen and understand.

It is a model that I have tried hard to adopt in the opportunities I have had in public debates and private conversations with academics, medics, activists and politicians in the public square. His concept of respectful dialogue has also had a major effect on the way I have tried to work and teach others as a doctor. I have tried to develop and popularise the concept of 'expert–expert relationships' as a model for doctor–patient and doctor–parent collaboration. It turns out that respectful, humble listening, careful dialogue and gentle persuasion can be an excellent, albeit countercultural, way to practise clinical medicine.

In the 1980s, as Stott's international ministry grew, he was inundated with invitations to speak and serve around the world. He called together a small group of close friends to advise him, of whom I was one. I was struck again by his humility and authenticity in his willingness to share his heart with us, his wholehearted longing to serve, his frustrations at not being able to respond to every request for help, and readiness to submit to our advice and recommendations.

Sharing vulnerabilities

As we spent time together, both with groups of other friends and alone, our friendship grew and I was struck by the degree to which he was willing to share his own vulnerability with me. In 1978, I was a newly qualified doctor and starting to explore possible future roles in medical service. I was still single and I remember a conversation we had in private about singleness. 'I'm wondering whether God is calling me to the single life, like you, Uncle John.' He replied with something like, 'I'm not sure that I would recommend it, dear brother.' And then, to my astonishment, he went on to talk about some of his struggles as a single man. The loneliness of coming home late at night to an empty flat, the temptations, the women who had 'set a cap' at him, the need to be constantly on his guard in case he was accused of inappropriate behaviour with a woman, the fact that he had no one to even give him a hug. He was in his fifties, a revered spiritual giant at the peak of his international ministry, and I was a twenty-six-year-old at the beginning of my career. I remember being astonished at his openness and vulnerability. And, on reflection, I was also aware that he was modelling humility and authenticity. He was showing that he trusted me and was moving our relationship on to a deeper, more intimate and more open level.

There have been particular moments in my own life, times of celebration and times of deep blackness, when his friendship has meant a great deal to me. One moment in particular still brings tears to my eyes as I think back to hearing his voice on the telephone. I was in deep despair and confusion having been admitted to a locked hospital ward following an acute psychiatric breakdown. 'I value your friendship, John,' he said. I was deeply moved that he had taken the trouble to track me down and make that call.

I've no doubt that experience brought us closer together when our roles were reversed some years later. John was admitted to hospital for emergency surgery following a serious fall and it was a great privilege for me to spend some time with him nearly every day during his hospital stay. Immediately following the surgery, he had periods of confusion and visual hallucinations which lasted for several days. Once staring across the hospital ward, he pronounced, 'I can see a forest stretching into the distance,' – pause – 'a *deciduous* forest.' His hallucinations caused him great concern as he feared he was permanently losing his mind, although at other times he was perfectly orientated and *compos mentis*. We laughed and wept together over the indignities and petty humiliations of hospital life, and the alarming frailty of our bodies and our brains.

On returning to his beloved bachelor flat in Bridford Mews, he was occasionally emotionally overwhelmed by the implications of his physical condition and his lost independence.[16] He was taken aback by the force of his emotions and struggled to understand himself. He was not prone to detailed self-analysis and, for most of his life, he tended to take his robust physical health and mental equanimity for granted. But the novel experience of 'blubbing together', as he irreverently called it, was moving and liberating, and it brought a new dimension of mutual vulnerability and openness to our relationship.

When he asked my advice on a medical matter, I remember teasing him that as a baby doctor I was completely useless. 'But I am very good on nappy rash.' 'I hope it hasn't come to that yet, dear brother.'

As we walked together towards the end, it was poignant to see how our relationship changed. He often talked personally about the reality of human frailty and of our utter dependence on God, the God who himself enters into the human experience of weakness and dependence. Once he shared with me his practice, when walking alone, of remembering that every fresh breath, every heartbeat, was a gift from God which could be taken at away at any time.

In his last book, *The Radical Disciple*, published in 2010, just one year before his death, his penultimate chapter was entitled 'Dependence'.

I sometimes hear old people say 'I don't want to be a burden to anyone else.' But this is wrong. We are all designed to be a burden to others. You are designed to be a burden to me and I am designed to be a burden to you. And the life of the family, including the life of the local church family, should be one of 'mutual burdensomeness'.[17]

But the practical reality of increasing physical dependence and memory loss wasn't at all easy for him to bear. As someone with a lifelong, razor-sharp intellect, he found the memory lapses and occasional confusions of old age painful and, at times, humiliating – although he rarely let on how much he felt the loss. With his usual self-deprecating sense of humour, he often made fun of his own 'decrepitude'.

Characteristically, he remained his own severest critic. During the period after his fall, while he was struggling to come to terms with the implications, I remember him saying to me that he was deeply disappointed that, 'after so many years of living as a Christian I am still capable of such self-preoccupation and selfishness.' He had always defined himself in terms of Christian service and the realisation that his public ministry was coming to an end was particularly painful for him. But he accepted his losses with Christian fortitude, with patience and with good humour. 'Like Paul, I am learning the secret of being content in every situation . . . I would not say that I am happy, but I am content.'

Towards the end, he found it increasingly difficult to find words for what he wanted to say. Sometimes it would take many minutes as he struggled to communicate a single thought. It was an extraordinarily painful loss for one who had been so fluent and articulate. I remember him struggling to articulate the words, 'Pray for me, John. Pray that I will die well.' When our friendship started thirty-five years previously, he would pray movingly for me as a young student, and now our roles were reversed. It was a tearful privilege to hold his hand and to try to find the heartfelt words for what he wanted to express but was incapable of articulating. Although his death in 2011 was long anticipated, I found it deeply shocking and disorientating; the sense of devastating loss was similar to that I had experienced at the sudden and unexpected death of my own father, years earlier.

As we have seen, the biblical model of friendship involves sharing our innermost heart. 'I no longer call you servants, because a servant does not know his master's business. Instead, I have called you friends, for everything that I learned from my Father I have made known to you' (John 15:15 NIV). Gospel-shaped friendship involves a sharing of the heart, of one's deepest thoughts, understanding, intentions, goals and longings. It's seen, astonishingly, in the intimacy of YHWH's friendship with Moses, 'The LORD would speak to Moses face to face, as one speaks to a friend' (Exodus 33:11 NIV).

And as his close friends spent time with John Stott, he shared his innermost heart with us. We saw his prayers, his longing for God's glory, his love for the Bible, his desire to be faithful to the truth, his confidence in God's goodness, his vision for the global church, and his heart for the poor, the vulnerable, the abused, the directionless and the lost. It's that level of sharing, of transparency, honesty and vulnerability, that changes lives. And now as I write these words in 2023, just fifty years from the time that I first met John Stott, I have no doubt that his friendship changed my life, and the lives of many. This is what transformative friendship looks like.

6

John Stott and his friends from across the world

Stott wrote very little about his own practice of friendship, but in his early book *Guard the Gospel* there is a brief reference.

> One sometimes meets super-spiritual people who claim that they never feel lonely and have no need of human friends, for the companionship of Christ satisfies all their needs. But human friendship is the loving provision of God for mankind . . . Wonderful as are both the presence of the Lord Jesus every day and the prospect of his coming on the last day, they are not intended to be a substitute for human friendships . . . When our spirit is lonely, we need friends . . . To admit this is not unspiritual; it is human.[1]

Near the end of his life, in an interview, John Stott was asked, 'When do you feel most alive?' The three things that he listed were public worship, enjoying nature and human friendships. 'I'm grateful to have many friends,' he said, 'and very grateful to have the opportunity to enjoy their friendship, and to do things with them.'[2]

It has often been remarked that, whereas friendships between women frequently involve prolonged face-to-face conversations, friendships between men are often centred around shared activities, 'doing things' together. Certainly, this was the case for many of Stott's friendships – shared Christian ministry, birdwatching trips, working parties at his retreat cottage in Wales, excursions to the cinema, concerts and restaurants. All of these were opportunities for enjoying and building friendships.

In this chapter I have recorded the words and stories of a small selection of Stott's friends from around the world. And through these words we can see a wide variety of gospel-shaped friendships in action.

David Zac Niringiye

Zac was a young Ugandan staff worker for a Christian student movement when he first met John Stott, who was speaking at an International Fellowship of Evangelical Students (IFES) meeting.

> Uncle John, as many of us his younger friends and mentees fondly called him, accompanied me throughout my adult life and ministry – from our first meeting in 1980, through face-to-face encounters, regular letter correspondence, and my listening to him at various conferences and closely studying his many books. In particular, I have two most cherished memories. First, during my time as a graduate student at Wheaton College, he was a featured speaker in chapel in 1987. He recognised and greeted me in the gathering, inviting me to the back room of the chapel to pray with him before he spoke, and then he asked that I pray for him. I thought for a moment. Me? Pray for world-renowned John Stott? I was deeply moved by his humility. Second, we spent time together on a ten-day birdwatching holiday in the wild and parks of Uganda in 1999. I was amazed at his authenticity – no airs about being a celebrated global evangelical icon – as we ate, drank and laughed together, discussing theology and ministry, as well as life's twists and turns.[3]

Zac told me that once John had shared with him, in private, a deep sense of personal hurt and bewilderment. A prominent Christian leader whom Stott counted as a friend had criticised him in public, accusing him of betraying biblical truth. 'He didn't even contact me first to warn me and ask whether he had misunderstood.' John Stott asked Zac to pray for him as he struggled with his own deep emotions of hurt and betrayal. His vulnerability, honesty and humility with the younger Ugandan Christian left a lasting impression.

So many of Stott's closest friendships were formed from apparently chance meetings as he travelled the world, and one of the most remarkable was his encounter with a teenage boy in Mexico.

Saúl Cruz

Saúl Cruz was a thirteen-year-old from Oaxaca, Mexico, when he was given the book *Cristianismo Básico* (*Basic Christianity* in Spanish translation).[4] He was captivated by it and prayed the prayer of commitment to Christ found at the end of the book. But the more he reread the book, the more questions filled his mind, questions that only the author could answer. He contacted the local IFES group and through them found John Stott's address in London, writing a letter with a long list of questions. Some weeks later he received a letter back from John's lifelong secretary Frances Whitehead, answering some of the questions but telling Saúl that John Stott was travelling shortly to Mexico and would be taking a service at a church in Mexico City, and giving him the date and address.

Determined to ask his questions, Saúl decided to hitchhike across Mexico to see the author of *Cristianismo Básico*. He arrived at the church travel-worn, just after the service started, took up position on a seat near the back and, having travelled through the night, promptly fell asleep. At the end of the service he tried to speak to John Stott, but in the crush was only able to greet him briefly. Disappointed, Saúl sat on a bench outside the church. After a few minutes, a car stopped next to him. It was John Stott and his hosts. Recognising Saúl, they invited him to join them for a meal at a local restaurant. Saúl remembered his bewilderment and joy at being placed close to John Stott and being able to ply him with questions. At the end of the meal, once it became apparent that Saúl had nowhere to stay in Mexico City, he was invited back to the host's house where John Stott was staying.

It was clearly an affluent family home. On retelling the story years later, Saúl remembered being struck by the immaculate white carpets and being embarrassed about his clothing and dirty shoes. But Stott took the young boy under his wing. 'Let's go and eat some ice cream.' More questions and earnest discussion. At the end of the evening, Saúl was ushered by the maid of the house to an upper bedroom. Stott joined him and said, 'Would you like to pray with me?' Saúl remembered kneeling at the bed alongside Stott, exquisitely conscious of his dirty shoes. At the end of the prayer, he hid his shoes under the bed, washed and fell asleep.

In the morning, Saúl woke up to find his shoes unaccountably clean and shiny. In his surprise, he asked the maid. 'Did you clean my shoes?' 'Certainly not,' she said. The hosts suggested that Saúl should ask Uncle John. Finally, the mystery was solved, 'Allow me to do this little service for you, my dear friend.'

Saúl went home that day excited and overjoyed. Just three years later, the seventeen-year-old Saúl was again in a meeting at which John Stott was speaking. Catching sight of him at the end of the meeting, Stott came over, greeting him with a warm hug, 'Saúl, my beloved friend.' And their friendship lasted and blossomed over the following forty years. In 1984, Saúl and his wife Pilar founded *Armonía*, a school for children with special needs which grew into a ministry of practical care and support for those living in urban and rural poverty in Mexico. In 1987, John Stott invited Saúl and Pilar to spend a term with him at the London Institute for Contemporary Christianity (LICC) and their friendship grew and deepened. 'Saúl, I pray for you every day,' Stott said.

In 1988, Saúl, Pilar and their children Eidi and Saúl Junior started a ministry in the Jalalpa Ravine, one of Mexico City's largest slums, establishing a community centre that was built on a garbage dump. Stott remained deeply involved in the work of *Armonía* and in the lives of all four members of the Cruz family. As Pilar Cruz put it, 'He was humble and open to learn and be blessed by others.' Eidi recalls how John treated her lovingly like his own granddaughter and how she was able to share her joys, struggles and giggles with him. Stott presented Saúl Junior with his precious youth Bible. The family remembered his warmth and love as he said, 'If I had five lives, one of them would be with *Armonía*'.

Ruth Padilla DeBorst

There's no doubt that the Latin American theologians René Padilla and Samuel Escobar had a remarkable influence on Stott's own thinking and ministry. Samuel Escobar, a fiery Peruvian theologian who became a close friend, was publicly critical of evangelicals who opposed the totalitarianism of the left but not that of the right, and who were blind to the evils perpetrated by Western governments and multinational corporations in the majority world. Stott had met the Ecuadorean theologian René Padilla through his connections with IFES and he became a lifelong friend and ally. As René's daughter Ruth put it, 'Their deep friendship exposed John to the social and political realities in which René and Samuel were honing their theological perspectives . . . John chose vulnerable engagement with his Latin American friends.'[5] Together they were crossing the barriers of race, class and background, embodying the values of the gospel in the way they lived together.

John stayed with the Padilla family in Buenos Aires in the early 1970s and Ruth helped as an interpreter in many of his conversations with visitors. 'He had a pastoral heart; a genuine concern for people and an interest in their individual stories and perspectives.' Later Ruth had a chance to sit with him while he was visiting Wheaton College. 'He chose to build a friendship with me. Later when acting as his interpreter in talks in Quito, John made me feel like the most accomplished translator in the world. "Ruthie," he endearingly called me, as only my closest family did.'

Ruth highlighted Stott's humility and generosity:

John Stott confounded the stereotypes of white Christian leaders. He was genuinely humble and generous. When René visited Stott in his tiny London flat, Stott insisted that René should take his bed while he slept on the couch. His giving and generous friendship recognised and affirmed the works of young radical Latin American Christians like Escobar and Padilla.

Years later, when Ruth's husband died in shocking and violent circumstances, she said that:

> His embrace stretched across the ocean . . . I was just so honoured to think that he would take the time to write a wonderful long handwritten letter to encourage me in my loss . . . He lived out love and authentic respect for people, a peace-granting and loving presence. It was God's mark on his life.

Vinoth Ramachandra

Vinoth is a Sri-Lankan theologian who first met John Stott as a student in London in the 1970s, and their friendship continued from those times to the end of Stott's life. Here are his words:

> Much of John Stott's 'British public school theology' was challenged by his visits to the non-Western world and his friendships with non-Western Christian leaders. He actually listened to us, unlike so many others who only came to propagate their views and to 'train' us. Commitment to the poor, and a growing engagement with social and political ethics, came to the fore in his later writings, much to the consternation of his conservative friends. His eclecticism and willingness to engage in dialogue with Roman Catholics alienated him from many in his own country who believed that there was nothing they could learn from others in the global body of Christ. When Stott invited me to give the London Lectures in Contemporary Christianity of 1998 (lectures which eventually became a book, *Faiths in Conflict? Christian Integrity in a Multicultural World*), he took me out to dinner to explain the aim of the lectures and urged me, 'Please help us evangelical Christians to see our blindspots.' Here was a seventy-seven-year-old man desiring to be taught by an obscure non-Westerner roughly half his age and with, hitherto, only two books to his credit! I was amazed. I have not met any other leader, before or since, who has expressed to me such a desire.[6]

Mercy Abraham Imondi

Mercy Abraham Imondi first met John Stott in 1994 when he went to India on a speaking trip.

I was in my early twenties and I had the opportunity to hear John speak at a seminar. Although most of the people there were older and more senior, I found myself sitting on the front row. At the time, I was struggling with loneliness and anxieties about my future. I had left my parents' home after university as I did not believe that God was calling me to the life expected of me by my family. I was estranged from my father and had not spoken to him for three years. I had heard God's call to care for abused and vulnerable young women and children in our community and so I had opened a women's refuge with fifteen young women staying in the home. But the locals thought it was a prostitute house and kept asking me to move on. At the end of the seminar, John Stott came over to me and sat beside me. 'I think there is something troubling you. Can you share with me what it is?' I explained the situation and that I was estranged from my father. John replied, 'If you would allow me, I would like you to think of me as your father from now on. And if you can find some land to build a women's refuge, I will purchase it for you'. When I found some land, he sent me £4,000. I was in my twenties, John was in his seventies, and this father–daughter relationship continued throughout the rest of John's life. His support, prayers and encouragement established me in my work which has continued for over thirty years.

The Mahalir Aran Trust in rural Tamil Nadu, South India, now houses about one hundred vulnerable and traumatised women and children, providing practical support, and medical, emotional and spiritual care.[7]

John was an encourager, a supporter, a friend and a father-like figure. He sent me frequent letters of encouragement (which I have kept), often repeating the words, 'I am like your father.' Through his encouragement All Souls Church sent a short-term mission team in 2002 to help build hostels for the women and children. He encouraged me to buy additional land and plant fruit trees to attract the birds. He was a role model who gave me inspiration to train and encourage young people and I have set up a missionary training programme for young people. After his death, he left me a substantial legacy and with that money we are building a community centre which will be used to train pastors and young people. It will be dedicated to his memory.

I once asked him, 'Uncle why do you love me so much?' His answer was that I had won his heart. I visited him a year before he died in his nursing home and he held my hand and said that he hoped someone would look after me when he died.

Mercy is now married to Vincenzo and they have an adult daughter.[8]

Mark Labberton

Mark Labberton was a study assistant for John Stott and subsequently returned to the USA, becoming President of Fuller Seminary.

Birdwatching trips with John involved a wonderful communion with him and with nature. There is no doubt that our communion with John was enhanced by our communion with the natural world. On these trips he was playful, worshipful, observant, joyful. John knows the way of birds and it's as though he's inviting me into a space in which he is completely comfortable, at ease, confident, but also a wide-eyed learner. He becomes an usher, a mentor, a guide. It's as though he was saying 'I'm introducing you to wonder.'

Mark, who spent many hours working for and travelling with John, also observed the breadth and depth of his friendships. 'He made emotional and relational space for other people. It was grace-based and free. There was compassion, love, care and thoughtfulness instead of power and domination.'[9]

Matthew Smith

Matthew was John Stott's study assistant from 2002 to 2005.

Since John Stott did not have his own immediate family, in his later years he took on a fatherly or avuncular role with many of his friends. He would take the initiative by writing personal letters to his friends around the world. When he was in London, he would spend an hour or so every day writing and dictating personal letters. He would ring people up on their birthdays or special anniversaries. His memory for details was phenomenal. He remembered the names of children, spouses and close relatives, dates and events. And his memory for details was based on his regular and disciplined prayer for each individual that he knew and loved.[10]

Rico Tice

Rico Tice became a curate at All Souls Church while John Stott was Rector Emeritus and they developed a close friendship which lasted right to the very end.

Uncle John's last lesson in service came for me on the day he died. There was a little bit of a rota amongst the staff to go down to his home, the College of St Barnabas in Lingfield, and it happened to be my day to go on 27 July. I took the train down that morning and got there at about 10 am. Frances Whitehead was sitting in the room, as was his beloved niece, Caroline. The doctors had told them that he was dying, and so having slipped out to ring Chris Wright, who was at a conference, I came back in and sat with him, and at one point I remember reading through John 14. He barely acknowledged me, but that was not the case when one of the Filipino cleaners from the College came in to say goodbye. He was a young man and had obviously heard that John was dying. With a monumental effort, John took his hand and rose up out of his bed to kiss it, and then slumped backwards. As I was leaving, Uncle John's inner circle began to arrive, but I noted that none of them were given anywhere near the greeting that he gave that young man. As I shut my eyes, I can see him giving everything he had to serve the person who had the lowest status. He was a Christian servant to his last breath and I'm so deeply grateful to God for his example.[11]

The following first-hand comments and observations about Stott are all taken from the book, *John Stott: A Portrait by His Friends*, edited by Chris Wright and published in 2011.[12]

Timothy Dudley-Smith

Timothy Dudley-Smith, former Bishop of Thetford and renowned hymn writer, was a lifelong friend of John Stott and wrote two definitive biographies about his life.

Dear John! How much we owe him! How different my own ministry would have been if he had not stopped me on the stairs all those years ago and known my name! When I was researching for the biography in London, while he was abroad or at the Hookses [his cottage in Wales], he would allow me to stay at his flat. As I browsed among his books and files I often found myself thanking God for all he has been to so many people . . . to visit him as I have done in his old age and infirmity at the College of St Barnabas is to come away with a surer sense of the unseen world of spiritual reality.[13]

Myra Chave-Jones

Myra Chave-Jones was an influential writer and speaker on psychology, grief and mental health issues. She met Stott at university and was a lifelong friend and confidant.

John was one of the most Christlike people I have ever known. His forbearance, patience, gentleness and genuine humility . . . and a thousand other fruits of the Spirit were well known to everyone and an abundant blessing to all of us.[14]

Frances Whitehead

Frances Whitehead was John Stott's personal secretary and close friend over many decades. She typed every word of his more than fifty books and probably knew the inside story of his life better than anyone else.

As I look back over the years, I can say without hesitation that my earliest impressions of John as a man of the utmost integrity have proved abundantly true. He was not only a brilliant Bible expositor but also one who sought constantly to live out what he believed and taught . . . I found John to be a true friend and a great man to work for and with.[15]

Ajith Fernando

Ajith Fernando was National Director of Youth for Christ in Sri Lanka for thirty-five years, and now continues his ministry as Teaching Director.

I was on the planning team for the Lausanne Younger Leaders Conference, Singapore, in 1987. There was no doubt that the hero of this conference was John Stott. But he distinguished himself by *not* speaking at it. He did give one short message, but he was there for the whole conference – over a week – just so that he could be an encouragement to the younger leaders. He devoted every spare moment to personal appointments with the delegates. It was clear that behind the greatness of this man as a communicator of Christian truth was a love for people and a commitment to personal ministry . . . My friend Peter Kusmic from Croatia tells how he once went to an airport chapel to pray. In the front of the chapel, he could see the head of an older man and scores of papers which he seemed to be arranging according to different categories. Upon closer observation he discovered that it was John arranging a huge pile of personal letters that he had written. I used to be amazed that he had time to write to me. Later l realised that if one is to have an international ministry, one must also have a ministry of international intercession and correspondence.[16]

Chris Wright

Chris Wright was Principal of All Nations Christian College and became International Ministries Director of the Langham Partnership International in 2001. An Old Testament scholar and prolific author, he has taken on and extended Stott's international speaking and teaching ministry. He edited *John Stott: A Portrait by His Friends*.

He had a rich reservoir of friendships around the world. I think that must be one of John Stott's greatest contributions to the world church – intangible though it is – his own unbounded capacity for genuine friendships all around the world multiplied and enriched whole new generations of consequential friendships among hundreds of others, some of them very dear and deep. It's a beautiful human legacy with God's fingerprints all over it.[17]

Peter Harris

In 1983, Peter Harris founded A Rocha, a global family of conservation organisations dedicated to creation care. John Stott was a lifelong supporter, friend and encourager of his ministry.

The simplicity of his lifestyle was a constant reminder of his many friends around the world who lived in tough and needy circumstances, and whom he always kept in his mind and in his (meticulously organised) praying. He was a great companion and a true Christian – probably more profoundly converted than anyone else I have known.[18]

7

Paul–Timothy friendships

In our earlier review of friendship in the Bible, there is an important example of intergenerational friendship that we have not yet looked at, that between Paul and Timothy. And there is no doubt that this intimate and heartfelt bond, described in considerable detail in the pages of the New Testament, had a special resonance for John Stott in the later years of his ministry.

As we focus on what we can learn from the New Testament writings about the deep bond between Paul and Timothy, we must of course acknowledge its uniqueness. Paul was an authorised apostle of the church who was passing on to Timothy an apostolic commission. No relationship today could possibly have the same awe-inspiring resonance. Yet the Paul–Timothy relationship has been used as a model for intergenerational Christian friendships for both men and women over the succeeding centuries and it is still relevant to us today.[1]

This was not lost on John Stott as he was writing his commentary on 1 Timothy in 1996. In his Author's Preface he writes:

It was as a comparatively young man that I began a serious study of the Pastoral Letters, so that I found no problem in sitting beside Timothy and Titus, listening through their ears to the elderly apostle's admonition. But now the situation has changed. I am almost certainly older than the apostle was, and it is natural for me to sit beside Paul. Not of course that I am an apostle. But I think I feel something of his concern for the future of the gospel and for the youngest generation whose responsibility it is to guard it and pass it on.[2]

Paul's relationship with Timothy

So let us 'sit beside' Paul and Timothy, whether male or female, and wherever we are on the journey. Let's try to think ourselves into their story. What can we learn about their friendship from the letters and other historical evidence preserved in the New Testament?

1 The friendship is intensely personal and heartfelt

Paul is nearing the end of his life and Timothy is still comparatively young. If he had been about twenty years old when Paul first enrolled him in the work of being a missionary, then at the time the Pastoral Letters were written, Timothy would be no older than thirty-five, still regarded as 'youthful' in the classical era. Paul describes Timothy as his 'genuine' or real child, using the Greek words *gnesio tekno* (1 Timothy 1:2). John Stott suggests that Paul might have been hinting at the circumstances of Timothy's birth.[3] Since his father was a Greek, Jewish law would have regarded him as illegitimate. But spiritually, Timothy was Paul's genuine child, partly because Paul was responsible for Timothy's conversion and partly because Timothy had faithfully followed his teaching and example.

In the second letter, Paul describes Timothy as his beloved child (*agapeto tekno*) (2 Timothy 1:2), assuring Timothy that he remembered him constantly in his prayers (v 3). Timothy had been moved to tears at their last parting, knowing that his much-loved spiritual father was facing execution. 'As I remember your tears, I long to see you, that I may be filled with joy' (v 4). 'I am reminded of your sincere faith' (v 5). And whenever I remember you Timothy, 'I thank God' (v 3).

Twice he appeals to Timothy to make every effort to come to see him in person. The intensity of the emotion is striking. This is no neutral or dispassionate relationship. Paul is an elderly, single man, under house arrest, aware that he is facing execution, and feeling abandoned by those such as Demas whom he had trusted (2 Timothy 4:10). 'At my first defence no one came to stand by me, but all deserted me' (4:16). He is longing to see his dear and faithful child face-to-face. But along with the intense emotion, there are also touchingly practical instructions. 'Do your best to come before winter' (4:21). 'When you come, bring the cloak that I left with Carpus at Troas, also the books and above all the parchments' (4:13).

There is no suggestion that Paul's relationship with Timothy was somehow exclusive, for Titus is also described as 'my true child in a common faith' (Titus 1:4). The letter to Titus shows that there were many similarities in Paul's relationships with the two younger men, although the relationship with Titus seems somewhat less intimate. But again, Paul pleads with Titus, 'do your best to come to me at Nicopolis, for I have decided to spend the winter there' (Titus 3:12).

And there is another touchingly intimate relationship revealed in the letter from Paul to Philemon. 'I, Paul, an old man and now a prisoner also for Christ Jesus – I appeal to you for my child, Onesimus, whose father I became in my imprisonment . . . I am sending him back to you, sending my very heart' (Philemon 9–12).

So there is no doubt that, despite its emotional intensity, the friendship between Paul and Timothy was not an exclusive bond. Instead, Paul had a rich network of heartfelt friendships with younger men, and from the evidence of Romans 16, with women as well, whom he regarded as spiritual children, but also as fellow workers in the gospel.

2 Paul recognises Timothy's Christian leadership potential

Paul had chosen Timothy because he saw his potential in Christian leadership. It seems likely that Timothy had heard the gospel from Paul and had been converted when Paul had visited Lystra on his first missionary journey. When Paul revisited Lystra a few years later, on his second missionary journey, Luke records that 'a disciple was there, named Timothy' who had clearly made progress in his Christian service and commitment: 'He was well spoken of by the brothers at Lystra and Iconium' (Acts 16:1, 2).

Paul's partnership with Timothy began during that second missionary journey, but it is clear that Timothy was already a known quantity. Luke tells us that he was the son of a mixed marriage, his father being Greek and his mother Eunice being a Jewish Christian (Acts 16:1). And we can conclude that there were three generations of believers in the family, since his grandmother Lois had also been converted to Christ (2 Timothy 1:5). So, Timothy had a track record. He came from a family with strong Christian commitments and had been acquainted with the Jewish Scriptures from childhood. In addition, he had been genuinely converted to Christ, was known publicly as a 'disciple' and had a good reputation among Christian believers in two different towns.

Paul also knew that the council of elders had laid their hands on Timothy and that he had been given a *charisma*, a grace-gift of the Holy Spirit for service in the body of Christ (1 Timothy 4:14, 2 Timothy 1:6). He saw the potential in this young man in his early twenties. Timothy had already demonstrated commitment to service, he had been approved and ordained by the eldership of his local church and he had some form of supernatural gifting.

3 Paul encourages Timothy to be faithful

Paul encourages and exhorts Timothy to be faithful to Christ, both in his public ministry and in his personal life. The Pastoral Letters are full of encouragement. Paul's passion for Christ and for the gospel overflows as he urges Timothy from the heart to be faithful. 'Wage the good warfare'(1 Timothy 1:18), 'train yourself for godliness' (4:7), 'set the believers an example in speech, in conduct, in love, in faith, in purity' (4:12). 'Keep a close watch on yourself and on the teaching' (4:16). 'Keep yourself pure' (5:22) and 'guard the deposit entrusted to you' (6:20).

In his letters, Paul moves seamlessly from public conduct as a church leader to private character and lifestyle. There is ultimately no division between issues of public and private life. In fact, there do not seem to be any 'no-go' areas in the correspondence. Paul moves from expounding profound doctrines of the faith to private sexual behaviour, relationships with church members, medical advice, spiritual warfare and personal heartaches.

It is the very ordinariness of much of the correspondence which has led some critical scholars to question its authenticity. And yet this intermingling of the profound and the prosaic seems utterly recognisable. This is precisely what an intimate conversation between friends is like, an interchange based on trust, openness and honesty. This is what it is like to share your deepest heart with another. And this is a genuine gospel-crafted friendship in all its richness, depth and ordinariness.

But it is striking that the pastoral letters contain no harsh criticism or rebuke for Timothy's failings. Instead, there is 'grace, mercy and peace from God the Father and Christ Jesus our Lord' (1 Timothy 1:2). Indeed, Paul describes Timothy, for all his youth and timidity, as a 'man of God' (6:11), encouraging him to 'continue in what you have learned and have firmly believed, knowing from whom you learned it' (2 Timothy 3:14).

If there is an element of rebuke in the letters, it is remarkably gentle and oblique. 'Don't be ashamed of the testimony about our Lord, nor of me his prisoner' (2 Timothy 1:8). 'Do not neglect the gift you have been given' (1 Timothy 4:14). And, the reminder that, 'God gave us a spirit not of fear but of power and love and self-control' (2 Timothy 1:7). The overall tone of the letters is of positive encouragement rather than criticism or reprimand. Paul, no doubt, had sensed that Timothy would respond much more positively to encouragement than to rebuke, and his love and regard for Timothy and for his heart of service overcame everything.

As he wrote to the Philippians:

I have no one like him, who will be genuinely concerned for your welfare. For they all seek their own interests, not those of Jesus Christ. But you know Timothy's proven worth, how as a son with a father he has served with me in the gospel. (Philippians 2:20–22)

4 Paul shares his heart and makes himself vulnerable

Despite his status as an apostle, a uniquely commissioned representative of the risen Lord Jesus, Paul opens his heart in private

107

to Timothy. Remarkably, he humbles himself before Timothy, reminding him of his own sins and failings.

> I thank him who has given me strength, Christ Jesus our Lord, because he judged me faithful, appointing me to his service, though formerly I was a blasphemer, persecutor, and insolent opponent. But I received mercy because I had acted ignorantly in unbelief, and the grace of our Lord overflowed for me with the faith and love that are in Christ Jesus.
> (1 Timothy 1:12–14)

Paul reveals his own vulnerability, his sense of betrayal by those close to him, his loneliness and his fears about the impending struggle:

> Remember Jesus Christ, risen from the dead, the offspring of David, as preached in my gospel, for which I am suffering, bound with chains as a criminal.
> (2 Timothy 2:8–9)

> You, however, have followed my teaching, my conduct, my aim in life, my faith, my patience, my love, my steadfastness, my persecutions and sufferings that happened to me at Antioch, at Iconium, and at Lystra –which persecutions I endured; yet from them all the Lord rescued me.
> For I am already being poured out as a drink offering, and the time of my departure has come.
> (2 Timothy 3:10–11, 4:6)

And as Paul chooses to expose the deepest thoughts of his heart, he also models a godly response to personal hurt:

> At my first defence no one supported me, but all deserted me; may it not be counted against them.
> (2 Timothy 4:16)

You are aware that all who are in Asia turned away from me, among whom are Phygelus and Hermogenes. May the Lord grant mercy to the household of Onesiphorus, for he often refreshed me and was not ashamed of my chains, but when he arrived in Rome he searched for me earnestly and found me – may the Lord grant him to find mercy from the Lord on that day!
(2 Timothy 1:15–18)

5 Long-term, committed, covenant loyalty

Paul commits himself to covenant loyalty in his relationship with Timothy, whatever the future might hold. The relationship between Paul and Timothy demonstrates the loyal love, the *chesed* of God himself. Both have committed themselves to each other, whatever might happen. Their friendship is based on face-to-face meetings when possible, regular correspondence and constant prayer:

I thank God whom I serve, as did my ancestors, with a clear conscience, as I remember you constantly in my prayers night and day. As I remember your tears, I long to see you, that I may be filled with joy.
(2 Timothy 1:3–4)

There is no sense that this relationship is just for a season, a time-limited mentoring arrangement that will come to an end. Instead, there is a covenant of loyalty that will bind the two men together until death.

6 A friendship which models support and instruction of others

Paul encourages Timothy to use their friendship as a model for supporting and teaching others. 'You then, my child, be strengthened by the grace that is in Christ Jesus, and what you have heard from me in the presence of many witnesses entrust to faithful men who will be able to teach others also' (2 Timothy 2:1–2). Paul expected and encouraged Timothy to seek out others, to look for those who were full of faith, those who could be trusted with the precious truths of the gospel and the Way of Christ. There seems little doubt that Paul was self-consciously recommending his friendship with Timothy as a future model for the spread and multiplication of the gospel.

Twenty-first-century, gospel-crafted, intergenerational relationships

So, what truths can we draw out from these primary sources about Paul's relationship with Timothy that can be applied to gospel-crafted intergenerational friendships in the twenty-first century? These are the principles that particularly strike me as we try to translate this ancient model of friendship into a contemporary guise.

1 A kingdom purpose

First, it's clear that the relationship had not developed by chance, nor was the friendship primarily a means to meet a lonely old man's desire for companionship. Of course, there was the human warmth and comfort of a father–son relationship. But there was also an intentionality, a kingdom purpose. As we have already seen, gospel-crafted friendships are framed within the context of gospel purposes, fostering growth and Christlike character, and fruitful Christian service. Paul had chosen to invest significant time, energy and resources in Timothy. It's not possible to know all the factors that had drawn Paul to the younger man. But as we have seen already, he has given a number of pointers in his letters. Timothy had a track record. He came from a family with strong Christian commitments, had been genuinely converted to Christ through Paul's ministry, was known publicly as a 'disciple', had a good reputation among Christian believers and had been ordained for ministry by a council of elders.

Paul could see Timothy's potential as a leader in future Christian ministry. And yet there are many hints that Timothy was not at all a conventional 'alpha male', an obviously impressive and naturally gifted candidate. Timothy is prone to timidity, he is at risk of being ashamed of Paul and of the gospel, and at risk of neglecting his spiritual gifts. He needs reminding and encouraging to fight the good fight, to live a life of purity, and to set the believers an example. The Paul–Timothy friendship reflects many of the paradoxes of Christian servant leadership. Instead of the common understanding (both then and now) that leadership must involve testosterone-fuelled dominion over others, the Paul–Timothy friendship models cross-shaped, sacrificial service for the other person.

As Jesus said:

> You know that the rulers of the Gentiles lord it over them, and their high officials exercise authority over them. Not so with you. Instead, whoever wants to become great among you must be your servant, and whoever wants to be first among you must be your slave – just as the Son of Man did not come to be served but to serve, and to give his life as a ransom for many. (Matthew 20:25–28 niv)

John Stott said more than once that those words, 'Not so with you,' should be underlined in red in every Christian's Bible.[4]

2 Focused on the transformation of heart and life

Second, the relationship is orientated towards a transformation of the heart and life. This comes out clearly in the pastoral letters. A characteristic of Paul–Timothy friendships is that they are focused primarily on fostering and encouraging internal spiritual growth, maturity and Christlikeness. There is also an element of teaching, discussion and advice about practical matters, but this is not at the core of the relationship. It is not a transactional agreement between two parties. 'I'll provide this service, and here's your side of the bargain.' It is heart-orientated rather than task-orientated. And hence it must be bathed in prayer, humility, honesty, sensitivity and mutual respect.

As one who has tried to play the role of Paul on a number of occasions, as I write these words, I am immediately aware of the awesome responsibility that we are taking on as an older friend and of my own personal limitations and failures. It is a truism of Christian leadership that we can only lead people as far as we have gone ourselves. And in the intimacy of a Paul–Timothy relationship, it is Christlikeness which is the most precious element. As many of John Stott's friends have said, his authenticity and Christlikeness were the most powerful and life-transforming aspects of his friendship.

3 Sharing heart and vision

Third, the relationship involves deep and intimate sharing of heart and vision. As we have seen, gospel-crafted friendships involve sharing of the heart, just as Jesus shared 'everything that I learned from my Father' (John 15:15). In other words, the relationship is profoundly self-revelatory and intimate. Jesus opened his heart to his friend–disciples, making himself intensely vulnerable before them. He wept with them, revealed his glory to the three on the mountain, shared his agony in Gethsemane and so on.

This is what deep friendship means in biblical terms, and it is almost shocking and disturbing in its intimacy and vulnerability. Is it really possible to experience this level of intimacy in our fallen human relationships? Or are the obvious risks and perils too great a price to pay? I will come back to these important questions about boundaries and safeguards in a subsequent chapter.

4 Intergenerational

Fourth, Paul–Timothy relationships are intergenerational. Here there is an obvious difference from the peer-to-peer friendships which seem to be much more common in our society. There is a natural difference between the older and the younger. The older friend is bringing life experience, wisdom, a history of service and ministry and by God's grace a personal knowledge of Christ. But they are also bringing, no doubt, a longer history of failures, weaknesses, sins and repentances. Their greater age and experience do not allow them to lord it over the other, but instead to serve them better.

James K. A. Smith provides a beautiful image:

> If you want to transcend time, build friendships across generations. Though you can't stand outside your own season, you can hear from those who've lived through your season. In my experience this is one of the great gifts of multigenerational friendships. Friendship in this respect is akin to time travel . . . if we can relinquish the myth of utter singularity, then listening to those generations ahead of us is a way of learning from our future. Granted, it is in the nature of youth to spurn such gifts, But when we are humbled, friendship across generations becomes a lifeline, an almost sacramental means of transcending the purview of our now as God gives us an outside glimpse of our moment. But the gifts traverse time both ways. Older generations attentively listening to those younger avail themselves of different ears to hear what's whispering or shouting now.[5]

And perhaps most importantly, there is a strong element of mutual respect between the generations. Paul does not only love Timothy, he respects him. He is not only 'my genuine child', 'my beloved child', he is also a 'man of God'. 'I have no one like him, who will be genuinely concerned for your welfare.' And Paul celebrates Timothy's 'proven worth, how as a son with a father he has served with me in the gospel.'

This is a notable feature of healthy Paul–Timothy relationships. Although they are intergenerational, they are not strongly hierarchical or authoritarian. The teaching and learning go in two directions. The older Christian has much to learn from the younger, as well as vice versa. They are two pilgrims learning together and walking together. They are both journeying together on the Way, and although one has been more years along the road than the other, they can support, encourage and learn from one another. There's fun, gentle teasing and sharing of everyday experiences. Just as in Paul's letters, deep intensity of emotion is juxtaposed with prosaic discussion of stomach difficulties and missing cloaks!

5 Strong boundaries – non-sexual and non-exclusive

Fifth, the friendship does have strong boundaries. In particular, it is non-sexual and non-exclusive. Between Paul and Timothy there was deep openness and intimacy. The two single men spent long hours alone and in private. Male homosexuality, particularly between an older man and a younger partner, was well known and even commonplace in the ancient world. Yet any hint of sexual intimacy or impropriety would have destroyed both Paul's and Timothy's reputations – Paul as an apostle of Christ and Timothy as an approved teacher of the gospel. Despite the intense emotion, closeness and tears in the relationship, there is no hint of inappropriate sexual intimacy.

Sexual issues are raised in several places in the epistles but Paul goes out of his way to urge Timothy to sexual purity, and cautions that his behaviour with women must not be misunderstood, 'Treat . . . older women as mothers, younger women as sisters, in absolute purity' (1 Timothy 5:1–2 NIV).

And similarly, there is no sense of exclusivity in the friendship. As mentioned earlier, Titus is also described as 'my genuine child in a common faith' and in Paul's old age, Onesimus became 'my very heart'. Despite its emotional intensity, the relationship between Paul and Timothy was not an exclusive bond. Instead, Paul had a complex network of individual and heartfelt friendships with both older and younger people whom he regarded as his spiritual children.

This is one of the wonders of friendship. The intimacy and depth of one relationship is in no way diluted by my friendship with another. In fact, as I learn and grow in one friendship, I develop greater abilities and resources for deepening friendships with others.

6 Open-ended and future-orientated

Finally, the friendship is open-ended and orientated to the future. When Paul decided to invest in Timothy, he had little idea where this relationship was headed. How would Timothy respond? How teachable would he be? Would he turn out to be an effective servant-leader? Or would he betray Paul's love and commitment, as so many others had?

Although it may seem to be an overly transactional idea, I find the concept of an investment is helpful. The investor has no idea of what the future may hold. He or she chooses to give their precious resources to another. It's a costly sacrifice and there is no certainty of any reward. Ultimately, the value of these costly time-consuming relationships will only be seen in the world to come. It is a hidden ministry of faith, hope and love, and these three virtues have eschatological overtones. We are pointing to the future.

Like all human relationships, intergenerational Paul–Timothy friendships may have a natural time-course. Sometimes it seems that the friendship becomes very close for a season and then there seems to be a natural waning of the intensity. In other cases, the friendship continues literally until the point of death. But by its very nature the relationship is open-ended.

It's important to remember that, of course, every friendship is unique. How could it not be? Although some common patterns can be discerned, there is no blueprint. A deep, intimate and revelatory relationship between two unique human beings will always have its own indefinable quality.

Here are at least some of the distinctive elements of Paul–Timothy friendships. As I reflect on the deep friendships that John Stott cultivated with many younger people, especially in his later years, it is obvious that he had learnt deeply from 'sitting beside Paul'. He shared Paul's concern for the future of the gospel and he chose intentionally to invest in many younger Timothys (of both genders) in order to encourage us, to share his heart with us, so that we might too guard and pass on the gospel of Christ.

Digressing for a moment, to John Stott's relationship with Nash, there is a revealing reference in Stott's commentary on 2 Timothy published in 1973. He wrote:

We have already seen that Paul was Timothy's spiritual 'father'. Having led him to Christ, however, he did not abandon or even forget him. No. He constantly 'remembered' him, as he says repeatedly in this passage . . . Such a Christian friendship, including the companionship, the letters and the prayers through which it was expressed, did not fail to have a powerful moulding effect on young Timothy, strengthening and sustaining him in his Christian life and service.

I thank God for the man who led me to Christ and for the extraordinary devotion with which he nurtured me in the early years of my Christian life. He wrote to me every week for, I think, seven years. He also prayed for me every day. I believe he still does. I can only begin to guess what I owe, under God, to such a faithful friend and pastor.[6]

I think it is helpful to see Paul–Timothy intergenerational friendships as merely a special case and example of gospel-crafted friendships in general. They operate under the same fundamental dynamics, they exhibit the same characteristics, the same logic. At their deepest levels, all gospel-crafted friendships have similar characteristics, however unique the expression. They reflect the wonderful and transformative logic of the gospel of Jesus Christ, and they breathe his love, joy, truth and humility.

The dangers of Paul–Timothy friendships

Just as these intergenerational friendships, when they express the love, authenticity and humility of the gospel, have such extraordinary power to transform lives for good, then perhaps it is not surprising that when they go wrong, they should also carry the potential for great evil. From the perspective of spiritual warfare, although many forms of friendship have been undermined and trivialised, it seems as though it is intergenerational friendships especially which have come under sustained attack over the last few decades.

Partly this is because intergenerational friendships are perceived as being out of tune with contemporary culture. For an older person to develop a close, intimate and committed friendship with a young person who is not a family member, can seem weird, creepy or downright predatory.

The tragic litany of 'spiritual abuse' scandals over the last decades have also demonstrated how close and intimate relationships between an older Christian leader and a younger person can frequently become the setting for the most damaging and egregious abuse. By their very nature, intergenerational friendships involve an imbalance of power, and hence there is an unavoidable potential for coercion, psychological control and manipulation.

The very existence of a power imbalance does not mean that abuse is inevitable. There was an extraordinary power imbalance between Jesus and his disciples, but he did not go on to abuse them. Instead, he emptied himself of his power and sacrificed his own interests to serve them. However, as broken and fallen human beings we have to recognise that whenever there is a power imbalance in our friendships, we need to take special care to avoid any element of abusive coercion and control.

We will return to this theme in greater detail in the following chapter but, first, I think it is helpful to compare and contrast Paul–Timothy friendships with other forms and patterns within the Christian community. In particular I would like to contrast this pattern of friendship with modern practices of 'discipling', mentoring, coaching and pastoral care.

As we have already seen, Jesus explicitly distanced himself from well-established patterns of rabbi–disciple relationship and discouraged his disciples from appropriating the title or the hierarchical customs of first-century rabbis.

But you are not to be called rabbi, for you have one teacher, and you are all brothers. And call no man your father on earth, for you have one Father, who is in heaven. Neither be called instructors, for you have one instructor, the Christ. The greatest among you shall be your servant. Whoever exalts himself will be humbled, and whoever humbles himself will be exalted.
(Matthew 23:8–12)

But this explicitly non-hierarchical and servant-minded model often seems to get lost in the relationships between older and younger Christians.

'Discipling' in contemporary Christian understanding

The use of the word 'discipling' for an activity that older Christians should undertake with those who are less mature has become commonplace in many segments of the Christian church. It is all too easy to say 'Jesus had twelve disciples. This was the way he changed the world. So we too should find disciples and pass on what we have learnt.' But this is precisely what Jesus told his disciples not to do!

Yes, we are called to 'make disciples' (Matthew 28:18) but I am not convinced that the concept of 'discipling others' is a helpful one. The word seems to carry overtones of hierarchy and authority. There is a very close link between the words 'discipling' and 'discipline'. In other words, the older Christian who is doing the 'discipling' naturally perceives that they have the authority and the duty to discipline and correct the younger, to exert their authority as a senior Christian over the junior person with the goal of curbing their sinfulness, waywardness, lack of commitment and so on. Although this process of correction may start with the best of motives it is easy to see how it can become abused.

In discipling someone, usually one far younger and more impressionable, a 'discipler' may come to take on a sense of personal responsibility for that person's progress in holiness. He or she presumes to exercise a role, which properly belongs to the Holy Spirit, to bring about personal transformation.

Mark Meynell illustrates what this might lead to:

For example, he might well discern arrogance in the young believer. That is certainly common enough! But then, the mentor assumes the role of sanctifier. This is not to exclude the place for a gentle challenge or even rebuke. Their effectiveness or expediency will often depend on factors such as the quality of trust between the pair, the mentor's ownership of his or her own sin, the younger believer's teachability and honesty. However, there is a fine line between a divinely appointed challenge and bringing someone 'down a peg or two.' Some of the tried and tested means included playing squash or tennis with the sole aim of resounding victory; or employing a harsh word or sarcastic put-down in a team meeting; or giving a deliberate cold shoulder for a period 'until he learned his lesson.'[7]

The ostensible reason for humiliating and demeaning the other is love, a desire to bring the younger to a greater obedience to Christ. But the bullying and abuse of power have consequences which are frequently catastrophic and lifelong. One of the characteristics of the so-called 'spiritual abuse' cases that have recently come to light is the systematic demeaning and humiliation of junior, powerless individuals within a spiritual context of so-called Christian 'discipling'. We will discuss this in greater detail in the following chapter.

Henri Nouwen points out that, in Christian leadership, it is often the inability to develop close and self-disclosing friendships that leads to the abuse of power:

> One thing is clear to me: the temptation of power is greatest when intimacy is a threat. Much Christian leadership is exercised by people who do not know how to develop healthy, intimate relationships and have opted for power and control instead. Many Christian empire-builders have been people unable to give and receive love.[8]

Mentoring and coaching

Mentoring has become one of the buzzwords of the twenty-first century and is now a very common idea within the Christian world. Just by way of example, an article in *Christianity Today*, entitled 'How to Be an Effective Mentor', explains the concept:

Why do the trades have apprenticeships and medical professions require internships? Because personal attention from experienced practitioners helps learners master essential skills, attitudes, and knowledge. This, of course, is no surprise to Christians familiar with the mentoring relationships of Moses and Joshua, Elijah and Elisha, Naomi and Ruth, Paul and Timothy, and Jesus and the disciples.[9]

The article goes on to explain that a mentor is 'a brain to pick, an ear to listen, and a push in the right direction,' as defined by the Uncommon Individual Foundation, an organisation devoted to mentoring research and training. It reports that 'mentoring is the third most powerful relationship for influencing human behaviour, after marriage and the extended family.'

It is said that the concept of 'mentoring' originated with the character of Mentor in Homer's *Odyssey*. Odysseus entrusted his young son Telemachus to the care of Mentor, his trusted companion, when he went away to war. Many authors make a historical link to the Middle Ages, when it became common practice for young people to take on apprenticeships in guilds and professions, often benefiting from the patronage of more experienced and established professionals. However, the modern understanding of the word 'mentoring' is surprisingly recent. It can be traced to the 1970s, when business people and researchers started to recognise the role of one-to-one coaching and training in the professional development of executives in large business corporations.

Coupled with the development of mentoring in large business corporations was a new focus on 'leadership training'. There was a rapid growth of research studies into the behaviour and practices of successful business leaders, and training courses were designed to instil similar characteristics into promising young business people.

Although similar to mentoring, professional coaching is usually regarded as a different form of training. Mentoring is based on a personalised approach to the client and does not include performance measures. Coaching is more standardised, and the coach applies performance measures to motivate improvement in the client and enhance their overall performance.

The origins of the modern coaching movement can also be traced to the 1970s. Coaching is described as a method of achieving set goals:

> The coach through dialogue helps the client to correctly set a goal, to find the best way to achieve the goal and reveal hidden inner potential in the client. The coach does not say how to achieve success, but asks questions through which the client themselves finds the solution to their own tasks.[10]

It's hardly surprising that the business concepts and practices of 'leadership training', 'mentoring' and 'coaching' should gradually move from the business world into Christian churches and organisations. The rationale seems obvious. 'Surely we can learn something from the practices of successful business executives which we can use for those who are leading large churches or large Christian organisations.' The basic idea is that leadership is a common human characteristic and skill and therefore the same principles and proficiencies will apply in all settings.

Of course, I immediately want to acknowledge that much that goes on under the heading of 'mentoring' or 'coaching' in Christian churches is very positive and helpful and in fact much closer to what I am calling 'gospel-crafted friendships', than to secular business practices. I certainly don't wish to be unduly critical or negative about a great deal of wonderful Christian ministry that is called 'mentoring' or 'discipleship training'. But I think it is helpful to dig down into the theory of mentoring and then ask how it relates to the Christian practices we see modelled in Jesus and in Paul.

As a business concept, the essence of mentoring is that it is primarily task-orientated rather than heart-orientated. It is focused on passing on skills and techniques. 'Let me show you how I do X.' 'This is the way to get round that technical difficulty.' Mentoring in its business context is clearly hierarchical. It would seem quite inappropriate for the mentee to try to teach anything to the mentor.

Professional mentoring relationships are also highly boundaried. It would be inappropriate for the mentor to talk about their personal struggles and emotions, and similarly, the mentee's personal problems which don't directly impinge on their work should not be brought into the relationship. Strong boundaries are seen as absolutely essential in professional and business mentoring relationships, in order to prevent any accusation of inappropriate intimacy, favouritism, blurring of roles or any issues with safeguarding.

In the business world, mentoring is not regarded as the same as friendship and the two concepts should not be confused. Similarly, mentoring should not be seen as counselling or pastoral support. A further important point is that mentoring is nearly always time-limited. 'I will agree to mentor you for a year, but afterwards you are on your own.' If one was to ask, what is the logic, the rationale of mentoring relationships, it seems fairly simple. At the risk of caricature, it would sound something like this: I am an expert in my business, a successful, highly trained, skilled practitioner. In comparison you are less skilled than I at the moment, but you clearly have promise. So, I am going to pass on my skills, my expertise, my understanding of the world, so that one day, you too may become a skilled practitioner. Of course, there is a place for various forms of hierarchical mentoring, or coaching, within the Christian church, focused on the passing on of particular skills, experience and insights. But I think we should draw a distinction between these modern business concepts and the biblical model of Paul–Timothy friendships, based on *mutual* support, love, transparency, vulnerability and encouragement.

Pastoral care

Traditionally, pastoral care in churches has been carried out by those in leadership positions. In many Protestant denominations the word 'pastor' (with its connotations of shepherding the flock) has been used synonymously with 'minister' or 'leader'. But increasingly there is a move towards an 'every member ministry' model of pastoral care where 'church members are encouraged to care for one another through small groups and the organic development of Christian friendship'.[11] This movement away from a highly professionalised model of pastoral care and towards member-to-member care within the church family has many positive aspects. But I think it is again helpful to recognise the differences between pastoral care and the model of friendship that we are discussing in this book.

The heart of pastoral care is providing godly, compassionate and wise support and assistance to individuals who are especially burdened by needs and difficulties. Inevitably, pastoral needs may be complex and multifaceted, and those providing pastoral support need the experience and skill to recognise the limits of their own competency and when to seek further help from other individuals and agencies. There is an inevitable power imbalance between the person who is needy and the one who comes alongside and, as a result, there is always a risk that this may lead to imbalances and distortions in the relationship, including various forms of emotional and physical co-dependency.

I am certainly not competent to discuss the many complexities and challenges which the provision of skilled pastoral care raises in the current climate of safeguarding concerns. This is a matter for other people who have specialist expertise. My aim is to point out how the biblical model of friendship differs from pastoral care. In particular, as I have stressed previously, this model of friendship is based on *mutual* support, openness and vulnerability. Inevitably, over the course of a long friendship, there will be seasons when one person may be more burdened and needy and the other is in a supporting role. But in a healthy friendship the support will never be only one-way. We are walking together and supporting one another along the Way, encouraging one another to become more fruitful in our service, more Christlike in our character, as we journey towards the final goal of joyful celebration and reunion in the house of the Lord.

As I have reflected on these issues, I have concluded that it may be helpful to conceive of a continuous spectrum in the nature of relationships. At one end are the relationships that are hierarchical and, to some extent, transactional – such as classical mentoring and coaching relationships. At the other end of the spectrum are the intimate, covenantal and mutual bonds that I am describing as gospel-crafted friendships. In reality, many friendships and relationships seem to fit somewhere between these two extremes and indeed they may move in one direction or another over time. It is certainly not my aim to be prescriptive or judgemental about the infinite variety of human relationships. However, I do think it is important for there to be some agreement on expectations, particularly at the more hierarchical and transactional end of the spectrum. If I am desperately seeking friendship and you are offering 'mentoring', there is an obvious potential for misunderstanding and hurt.

Friendships with those who don't share our faith

To what extent is it possible to develop deep and intimate gospel-crafted friendships with those who are not Christian believers? It's a profound and complex question which inevitably raises a host of new issues. I'm not qualified to explore these areas in any depth but can only outline a few fairly obvious headlines.

Friendship is part of the goodness of creation order and it's immediately obvious that deep, intimate, loving and covenantal friendships can develop between those of all faiths and none. From the perspective of common grace, we may be able to say that God is at work in all loving, covenantal friendships, although frequently hidden and unrecognised.

Speaking personally, I am immensely grateful for the privilege of a number of deep and significant friendships that developed over the years with people who didn't share my Christian faith, particularly with a number of my colleagues at work. Spending many hours working closely together in a pressurised intensive care environment, we built deep relationships of trust, mutual support and enjoyment.

Indeed, for some people, our friendships with non-believers may seem closer and more intimate than with fellow believers. But my experience is that when my friend does not share my Christian faith, there are always some very significant aspects of my life that I find difficult to disclose. One close friend and work colleague said to me that whenever I talked about my faith, 'It's as though you start talking a foreign language that I can't understand.' Since the biblical model of friendship focuses on sharing our heart, giving and receiving back the deepest and most significant parts of our lives, then despite opening ourselves to our friends there may well be 'no-go' areas that remain out of reach. But as we grow in the depth of our friendship, we continue to pray and long for the opportunity to share what we have discovered, 'one beggar telling another beggar where to find bread'.[12]

In the next chapter, we turn to look at how friendships, which can be such a powerful and joyful force for good, can also become twisted and broken by evil.

8

How friendships go wrong

We saw in an earlier chapter how the 'masters of suspicion', Freud, Marx and Nietzsche, had contributed to the current view that sex and power lie at the heart of all close bonds between people. We are now much more aware than we used to be that although healthy, gospel-crafted friendships remain the ideal for which we should strive, the powerful hidden forces of sex and emotional coercion and control are capable of distorting and ultimately destroying intimate relationships within the Christian community, with incalculable negative consequences for abused individuals and for the kingdom. Although all deep friendships can be distorted and deformed by these forces, it seems that it is particularly intergenerational relationships that are at risk. So in this chapter, my main focus will be on intergenerational friendships, although the same principles apply to other close and intimate bonds.

The last decades have seen a catalogue of abuse scandals implicating highly respected and prominent Christian leaders, nearly all of them male, and coming from every wing of the Christian church. It is striking that many of those implicated have been outwardly charming, gifted, persuasive and apparently 'spiritual' individuals. But each one was involved in abusive relationships with those who were under their influence. As the allegations of abuse were investigated, it became apparent that, although this is absolutely no excuse for their abusive behaviour, these 'charming and gifted' men had deep, hidden psychological and emotional needs and were broken. And they used their spiritual and psychological authority as Christian leaders to gratify their hidden needs for coercion, control, manipulation and sexual gratification.

The abuse perpetrated by Christian leaders has lifelong emotional and spiritual consequences for victims. And the scandals seem to confirm the 'hermeneutic of suspicion'. Perhaps Freud and Nietzsche were right. Perhaps in a broken and fallen world, close and intimate friendships outside marriage are just too dangerous, too open to misunderstanding and accusations of abuse. But if we allow mistrust and suspicion to prevent gospel-centred friendships then we allow evil to have the final word!

This is a complex and painful topic, and again I do not claim any special expertise or experience in the management of so-called 'spiritual abuse'. In light of that fact, I have referenced a number of resources on the topic that I have found helpful at the end of this book. However, if we are going to reimagine gospel-crafted friendships here in the twenty-first century, then it seems essential that we understand at least the basics of how intimate friendships can go wrong, and what red flags should raise concerns.

Spiritual abuse

Spiritual abuse is a special form of psychological and emotional abuse. It refers to an emotionally coercive and controlling abusive relationship which has special features because it is within the context of a church or spiritual authority. According to the definition provided by Dr Lisa Oakley, a recognised expert in the field:

> The target experiences spiritual abuse as a deeply emotional personal attack. This abuse may include: manipulation and exploitation, enforced accountability, censorship of decision making, requirements for secrecy and silence, pressure to conform, misuse of scripture or using the pulpit to control behaviour, requirement of obedience to the abuser, the suggestion that the abuser has a 'divine' position, isolation from others, especially those external to the abusive context.[1]

I have found it helpful to look at how a modern understanding of coercive and controlling abuse has developed over the last fifty or so years. In particular, there is the remarkable research carried out by the social scientist Albert Biderman among American airmen. During the Korean War in the early 1950s, the American military were deeply disturbed by the dissemination of a number of false confessions by US airmen who had been captured and imprisoned in facilities run by Chinese Communists. What devious psychological brainwashing techniques had the Communist guards used to manipulate those young American servicemen to betray their country?

Albert Biderman was commissioned to investigate the techniques employed by the guards. He interviewed 235 American servicemen who had been imprisoned by Chinese Communists during the Korean War and subsequently released. Approximately half of them had personal experience of attempts by prison guards to extort false confessions. The results of the study were published in 1957 in an influential paper entitled, 'Communist Attempts to Elicit False Confessions from Air Force Prisoners of War.'[2]

Biderman concluded that the prison guards adopted a common pattern of behaviour, which he described as 'essentially a teaching procedure' intended to break resistance and induce compliance in the prisoner. In the paper, Biderman listed eight common features which emerged from the interviews. I have listed them below in detail because, since Biderman's ground-breaking study, these features have been recognised as consistent and recurring elements in different cases of emotional and psychological abuse. These are the complex and subtle ways in which powerful individuals can weave a web of abuse and manipulation over their victims.

1 Isolation

Isolation has the effect of depriving the victim of social support from others, enabling the abuser to project a distorted version of reality and emphasising the dependence of the victim on the abuser. In the context of abusive friendship, the abuser may seek to prevent the victim from talking to others and seeking support outside the relationship: I am your special friend. You mustn't tell anyone else about what happens between us. I don't want you spending time with those other people. God has given me special authority over you. You must be loyal to me because, after all, you belong to me.

2 Monopolisation of perception

The abuser attempts to monopolise the attention of the victim, stopping them from focusing on distracting issues or developing interests and friendships elsewhere. This can lead to a kind of brainwashing – sometimes described as 'gaslighting'. This may involve planting false memories, questioning the victim's grip on reality, denying responsibility for harmful actions, shifting the blame onto others, and so on. The aim is to confuse and disempower the victim so that they can be manipulated and coerced.

3 Induced debilitation and exhaustion

In the context of physical imprisonment, the use of starvation, extreme cold and sleep deprivation is of course well known. In the context of emotional abuse, the debilitation is much more subtle, but may include bombarding the victim with demands, phone calls, texts, messages and constant interruptions in order to break down resistance and render the victim susceptible to control and coercion.

4 Threats

The abuser creates a climate of fear, threat and uncertainty, aimed at inducing high levels of anxiety and breaking down resilience. Often the threat is vague but menacing. 'If you don't do what I want, I am afraid that unfortunate things may happen.' 'Don't force me to do this.' There may be threats to reveal secrets about the victim, to humiliate them in public, to wound loved ones and relatives. The abuser may claim the authority of God for his words and actions, and may threaten the victim with spiritual judgement if they resist. 'You will be under the judgement of God if you do not do as I say.'

Mark Stibbe gave a chilling description of the way that the serial abuser John Smyth employed the threat of rejection to enforce control over his victims:

He employed classic 'inner ring' tactics, as described so eloquently by C. S. Lewis, 'It would be so terrible to see that other man's face – that genial, confidential, delightfully sophisticated face – turn suddenly cold and contemptuous, to know that you had been tried for the Inner Ring and rejected.' Reading that now, especially the description of the face of the one exercising the coercion, sends shivers down my spine. It is a perfect description of Smyth. As a spiritual leader, he presented a warm and genial face to me while I was conforming to his teaching. I knew that rebelling in any way against his views would mean rejection. He played on this fear we all had of his face turning suddenly 'cold and contemptuous'.[3]

5 Occasional indulgences

Many of the prisoners of the Communists described sudden oscillations between threats or actual torture, and the promise of favours and rewards from the prison guards. In the context of abusive friendships, this behaviour may often involve paying extravagant compliments to the victim, offering treats, carrying out a 'charm offensive', sometimes described as 'love bombing'. In a spiritual context, this may take the form of spiritual flattery, 'I really believe that you are a remarkably spiritual person. God is going to bless you in a very special way.' The excessive affirmation and flattery can represent a form of 'grooming' which is analogous to that seen in child sexual abuse. But flattery and charm may give way suddenly to hostility, threats and anger, when the abuser does not get his way. The oscillation between treats and threats leads to emotional disorientation and a sense of helplessness in the victim.

6 Demonstrating 'omnipotence'

The abuser shows off their power, knowledge and control over the victim in order to illustrate the futility of resistance. In a spiritual context, the abuser may demonstrate their theological knowledge and spiritual 'authority' over the victim. 'God has put me over you as your spiritual father.' Scripture is often quoted as a means of reinforcing the authority of the abuser. A frequent scripture used to justify abuse is Hebrews 13:17, 'Obey your leaders and submit to them, for they are keeping watch over your souls, as those who will have to give an account.' Obedience must be both total and unquestioning. Claiming the authority of a spiritual father, the abuser may insist on a relationship of ruthless accountability. He may undertake invasive questioning about personal sins and failures and insist on giving some form of physical or emotional chastisement for the 'sins' that have been extorted from the victim.

7 Degradation

The abuser continually demeans, insults, humiliates and degrades the victim, in order to imply that they are worthless and of little significance apart from the beneficent care and protection of the abuser. Public shaming and humiliation can form part of the arsenal of tactics. The aim is to extinguish any residual self-respect and destroy the ability of the victim to exercise their own will or challenge the authority of the abuser.

8 Enforcing trivial demands

The abuser demonstrates their control over the victim by continually demanding that they undertake trivial tasks or chores, or keep to meaningless rules. There may be rigorous demands on church attendance, commitment to weekday meetings, and so on. The abuser may enforce rigid spiritual practices such as spending specific amounts of time every day in spiritual disciplines such as personal prayer and Bible reading.

No abuser goes on a training course in order to inform themselves about Biderman's eight features of coercive control. And yet it is striking how frequently the accounts of abusive relationships within the context of church leadership reveal these same characteristics. And, as we have noted previously, it is relationships in which there is a marked power imbalance between the parties that are most at risk of emotional coercive control and manipulation.

It is not always the older and more senior person in the relationship who takes on a coercive and abusive role. Under certain circumstances, it is possible for the younger person to exert manipulative control over the older. But the relationships which are at particular risk of coercive control are those between an older, high-status individual who is perceived as having spiritual authority and influence, and a younger person who wishes to learn and grow and who is open to influence and suggestion. In other words, Paul and Timothy!

So here is the terrible irony. It seems it is precisely those intergenerational friendships which have the most transformative potential for good which are, at the same time, most at risk of facilitating evil. We cannot and must not ignore what we have learnt about the risks of abuse. Instead, we need to develop new ways of fostering and encouraging *healthy* intergenerational friendships that take into account the tragic realities that the last decades have taught us. Our goal is to foster and encourage the development and nurturing of gospel-crafted friendships that are *healthy, transparent, accountable and safe*.

Boundaries

Our aim should be that all deep and intimate friendships that take place in the context of the local church or other Christian communities do not expose anyone to risk of substantial harm. We want to encourage friendships that are safe, transparent and free, and in order to achieve this we must recognise and respect the three boundaries that we came across in an earlier chapter. These are the essential 'rules of the road' we should follow in developing friendships wisely and creatively. Healthy gospel-crafted friendships should be non-sexual; non-abusive, non-coercive and non-manipulative; and non-exclusive.

As we noted previously, these boundaries are not arbitrary; they come out of the essential nature of the gospel. They are necessary in order to protect the integrity of the individuals concerned and to ensure that, as far as possible, the friendship is safe, that neither person is at risk of coming to harm, and that these precious intergenerational friendships do not go wrong.

1 Non-sexual

Gospel-crafted friendships are based on deep and intimate love – but it is totally non-sexual love. Of course, sexuality is part of our created human nature and healthy Christian living does not involve the denial or repression of our sexuality (as Freud misleadingly taught). Instead, we are called to acknowledge our own sexuality, while maintaining a discipline of sexual purity in our interactions with one another.

Paul recognised the possibility that Timothy's pastoral relationships within the church might become distorted by sexualisation. So, as we have seen, he exhorted Timothy to 'Treat younger men as brothers, older women as mothers, and younger women as sisters, with absolute purity' (1 Timothy 5:1–2 NIV). Although it may seem rather jarring, perhaps we can say that to allow a sexual element to develop in Christian friendships can be as inappropriate in that context as it would be within a biological family.

The non-sexual boundary includes both any form of physical, sexual intimacy, and also sexual or romantic fantasies, or any form of sexual gratification which arises out of the friendship. Although it is obvious that deep male–female friendships have a potential for becoming sexualised, the last decades have taught us that same-sex friendships, both male–male and female–female, also have a potential for the development of inappropriate sexual intimacy.

As I stressed before, the non-sexual boundary does not mean that any kind of physical contact is forbidden or unwise. We are created as physical, embodied beings and particularly when we are in distress or lonely, we need to experience God's love in a physical form. We need a human touch, a warm hug, holding hands, hearing loving words. This is the way that God made us, to express and receive God's invisible love in a physical form. Some of the most moving and significant times in my friendships with John Stott and with my other closest friends have been expressed in a physical embrace.

Is it wise to develop close non-sexual friendships with people of the opposite gender, or should we stick to same-gender friendships?

In discussing this complex question with others, there appears to be a clear generational divide. Most Christians of the older generation will adhere to the traditional view that developing close friendships with people of the opposite gender is unwise and fraught with risk of sexual compromise and disaster. There are frequent accounts of male pastors developing inappropriate romantic and sexual relationships with women in pastoral contexts.

But, in general, I have found that younger Christians, while they are by no means unaware of the risks, are much more open to friendships across the genders. Much of this is because we are now so much more aware of the reality and ubiquity of same-sex attraction. It is simply not true that male–female friendships are at risk of sexualisation while male–male and female–female friendships are not. Every close and intimate friendship has the possibility of becoming influenced or distorted by a sexual or romantic element.

And there is an obvious inconsistency in the traditional view. When it comes to Christians who are same-sex attracted but living a celibate lifestyle, we do not strongly advise them only to develop close friendships with people of the opposite gender! Instead, we teach about the importance of openness, honesty and transparency in friendships.

So how do we prevent a sexual element from entering into our deepest friendships? Surely the most effective protection is to walk in the light with one another. The first and foundational characteristic of gospel-crafted friendships is that they are truthful, transparent and non-deceptive. We can maintain that essential boundary by being honest with ourselves and honest with one another, by *agreeing together* on the non-sexual nature of the friendship, however deep, intimate and self-disclosing it becomes. In many of our intimate friendships, this can be assumed without the need for discussion, but if there is any possibility of misunderstanding then it is surely much better to discuss the issue openly, however difficult or embarrassing this may be. Obvious practical precautions such as meeting in a public environment, such as a coffee shop, or in the presence of other friends, and avoiding potentially compromising settings, such as bedrooms, seem sensible. The historic abuse scandals demonstrate that abusers usually seek an element of secrecy in which to perpetrate their crimes, and this contrasts markedly with the openness and transparency of the gospel. Often the wisdom and advice of other friends can guide us as we navigate the complexities of maintaining sexual purity in relationships.

This is one area in which the friendship practices of John Stott and his generation of male Christian leaders might seem rather unwise, especially in the light of more recent abuse revelations. Although they were very concerned never to be alone and unsupervised with a woman who was not their wife or family member, when it came to friendships with men of all ages, that generation of leaders seemed largely oblivious to the risks of a sexual element arising. We live in a very different age and social context and so we need to 'reimagine' Christian friendship for the twenty-first century.

For those who are married, it is important that the marriage partner is aware and comfortable with the development of any close friendships. One wise rule is 'Don't say anything to your friend that you have not said to your spouse first.'

Would it be possible for a single man and a single woman to start a non-sexual friendship but then for a romantic and sexual element to enter into the relationship? Yes, of course it is possible. But once one or both become aware of this, it seems to me that they should walk in the light with each other and discuss where the relationship is headed. In Christian thinking, there is a clear line between non-sexual friendship and an exclusive, romantic relationship that leads to physical sexual expression in marriage. Because of the tragic consequences of sexualised relationships and, in particular, of any form of sexual abuse, we must not allow this essential distinction to become blurred. I recognise of course that this is a complex and difficult topic and I can only touch on the basic principles here. More detailed discussion can be found in the resources on spiritual abuse referenced at the end of the book.

2 Non-abusive, non-coercive and non-manipulative

The essence of gospel-shaped friendships is that they reflect the freedom of the gospel and are based on genuine respect for the other person. Sadly, as we have seen, it is all too common for a controlling or abusive element to enter relationships between older Christians (usually men) who are perceived as high-status and influential leaders and younger Christians who are open to suggestion and influence. In many cases, it seems that the older Christian did not start their ministry with a desire to abuse and coerce their victims. Rather, there was a gradual slippery slope of increasingly abusive behaviour.

The term 'spiritual abuse' is now widely used but it has also become contested and controversial. Other terms such as 'pastoral malpractice', 'religious abuse' and 'abuse of power' are increasingly employed. But, whatever language we use, it is clear that the majority of the recently highlighted abuse scandals within the Christian church involved leaders who adopted an attractive and apparently 'spiritual' *persona* but who abused their power over vulnerable individuals to gratify their own needs.

The more we recognise what healthy, transparent and respectful friendships look like, the more easily we will be able to identify behaviours and practices that are unhealthy and potentially abusive. As a respected older Christian leader once advised me, 'we need to teach and model the foundations of Christian truth, so that errors become self-evident.' That's why in this book I have tried to focus most of my attention on the positive and transformative aspects of deep and intimate friendships.

At the same time, it is surely essential that all those who are engaged in intergenerational friendships, whether older or younger, should be well informed about the risks of a coercive and controlling element entering the relationship, and be aware of the red flags to look out for. A frequent feature of 'spiritual abuse' is a coercive demand for 'accountability' under the guise of spiritual care and leadership. The victim is told that they must share every aspect of their life, behaviour, thoughts and temptations so that they can be scrutinised by the more powerful leader.

In their helpful book, *Escaping the Maze of Spiritual Abuse*, Lisa Oakley and Justin Humphreys list the key characteristics of coercion and control in a religious context, and the red flags to watch out for:[4]

- manipulation, pressure and exploitation
- expectation of excessive commitment and conformity
- enforced accountability
- censorship (including the inability to ask questions, disagree and raise concerns)
- requirement for obedience
- fear
- isolation and rejection
- public shaming and humiliation.

The authors emphasise the aspects of abuse specific to a religious, pastoral context, which include:

- the use of Scripture to coerce and control
- the claiming of a divine calling to aid coercion
- use of God's name or will to coerce
- threats of spiritual consequences or judgement for disobedience.

A frequent refrain of victims of spiritual abuse is that they were unaware of the possibility of psychological and emotional manipulation. They assumed that since the abuser was a well-known and respected Christian leader, then whatever happened must be 'godly' and 'normal'. They learnt to suppress their intuitive sense that something was wrong.

Perhaps one of the lessons we have to learn is that our intuitions may well be correct. Of course, intuitions can be misguided and unreliable too, but a sense of discomfort or unease about a close friendship should not be disregarded. If this is in the context of a church or Christian community, it is important that there are clear channels through which confidential safeguarding concerns can be communicated, and appropriate action taken.

What steps can older friends and leaders take to minimise the risk of a coercive, controlling element entering their friendships? First, we need to examine our motives for wishing to develop intergenerational friendships. Are we genuinely concerned for the good of the younger friend, hoping to encourage them in Christlikeness and godly behaviour, or do we have some selfish and self-regarding motivation? Do we genuinely wish to respect the integrity and freedom of the other, or is there a hidden desire to control and dominate their thinking and their behaviour? Are we genuinely interested to learn humbly from the other, to listen as well as to speak?

At the same time, it is important that we recognise our own vulnerabilities and weaknesses. Godly Christian leadership involves the wise and humble use of power.[5] Where I am at risk of using power in an ungodly way? What are my besetting sins and weaknesses and how might they be expressed in a close relationship in which there is an imbalance of power? What are my own character flaws and blindspots, and what steps can I take to ensure that they do not distort or damage my friendships?

As we become more aware of the risks of a coercive and controlling element entering our friendships, we can take practical steps to reduce them. We should avoid any tendency to dominate the relationship or insist on regular meetings or the completion of tasks. Freedom, gentleness and respect are the hallmarks of healthy friendships. We should make it plain that our friends are free to disagree with us and make space for them to express contrary opinions and ideas. Instead of demanding a high level of loyalty and emotional intensity, perhaps we should allow the younger friend to choose how often they wish to meet and to set the level of intimacy and self-disclosure that they feel comfortable with.

In addition to self-reflection about our friendships, it is very helpful to develop accountability structures with other older Christians who have experience of intergenerational friendships. By meeting regularly and discussing any issues raised in a confidential setting, while protecting the identity of the individuals involved, we help provide the transparency and accountability that are essential to ensure the safety of all concerned.

3 Non-exclusive

Isolation was the first coercive tactic identified by Biderman. By separating the victim from other social contacts, isolation facilitates the projection of a distorted version of reality and emphasises the dependence of the victim. One of the red flags we should look out for is a strong emphasis on secrecy and confidentiality. 'I don't want you to talk to anyone else about what I say to you.' 'I want you to be completely loyal to me.' 'What we do together is just between us.'

Children who are at risk of physical or sexual abuse are often instructed about the difference between 'good secrets' and 'bad secrets'. 'Bad secrets' are when there is an attempt to conceal that abuse is occurring or at risk of occurring. Similarly, when there is the possibility of abusive emotional coercion and control in relationships between adults, we need to reflect on the difference between good secrets and bad secrets. There is an appropriate place for confidentiality within intergenerational friendships, but if there is a risk of abuse leading to significant harm, then we should share our concerns with an appropriate person, such as a safeguarding lead, to enable a discussion about what action should be taken.

But even without an abusive element, exclusivity in a friendship tends to encourage an unhealthy co-dependency which fosters immature patterns of behaviour and inhibits genuine growth and spiritual formation. By their very nature, gospel-shaped friendships are non-exclusive. They do not exclude and separate out from others. Instead, as we have seen before, healthy friendships positively encourage and delight in drawing other people into the joy and openness of what they have discovered.

I close this chapter by reflecting again on the paradoxical reality that friendships that express the love, authenticity and humility of the gospel have such extraordinary power to transform lives for good. And yet, at the same time, they carry such potential for abuse and great evil. From the perspective of spiritual warfare, it seems as though it is intergenerational friendships in particular which have come under sustained attack over the last few decades. But instead of retreating into self-protective isolation, our aim must be to learn how to *reimagine* how these precious and transformative friendships can flourish and develop in the suspicious and jaded climate of the twenty-first century. But first we head back briefly to the eighteenth and early nineteenth century to see the central role of friendship in a remarkable period of evangelical resurgence in Britain.

9

Simeon, Newton and Wilberforce – the lasting impact of friendship among evangelicals

We've spent a long time looking at the dark side of friendship. As we come towards the end of our journey it's time to remind ourselves of the wonderful, liberating and joyful reality of gospel-shaped friendships and the way that, by God's grace, they are capable of transforming not only individual lives but wider communities and even society as a whole. The purpose of this chapter is to provide a brief historical snapshot of the central importance of a close network of friendships that lay behind a period of remarkable growth in the evangelical Christian faith in the late eighteenth and early nineteenth centuries.

On the wall of the staircase of John Stott's tiny flat was a small engraving of an immaculately dressed clergyman walking in a determined manner with a folded umbrella under his arm. I had often noticed this picture as I went up and down those familiar stairs. It was, of course, a portrait of Charles Simeon, rector of Holy Trinity Church in Cambridge from 1782 until his death in 1836. Simeon, a lifelong friend of William Wilberforce and John Newton, had been a key figure in the evangelical awakening at the time, and in John Stott's own words was 'one of the greatest and most persuasive preachers the Church of England has ever known.'[1]

It is well known that Simeon's remarkable and fruitful ministry in Cambridge, especially among students and future leaders, provided a model from which Stott learnt many lessons. For an anthology of Simeon's sermons, published in 1986, John Stott wrote a detailed Introduction.

It was during my undergraduate days at Cambridge University that I was introduced to Charles Simeon ... Simeon's uncompromising commitment to Scripture, as the Word of God to be obeyed and expounded, captured my admiration and has held it ever since. On many occasions I have had the privilege of preaching from his pulpit in Holy Trinity Church, and standing where he stood, have prayed for a measure of his outstanding faithfulness.[2]

Stott went on to list five characteristics of Simeon's life which were 'the secrets of his effectiveness as a preacher', namely, a personal faith in Christ crucified, a willingness to suffer for what he believed, thoughtful faithfulness to Scripture, a complete dedication to the ministry of preaching and his 'unalloyed personal authenticity'. 'There was no dichotomy between the man and his message, between the person and the preacher. There was nothing devious about him. He was a transparent Christian, who hated humbug.'[3]

There is no doubt that Charles Simeon's model, as a faithful and highly effective biblical preacher, was hugely influential on Stott's own ministry. But I suspect that Simeon's example, as a lifelong bachelor who saw the central importance of investing in friendships with students and young people, was also highly formative. Simeon held weekly meetings for undergraduate students in his rooms in King's College, Cambridge, and many of those who attended spoke subsequently of the impact of Simeon's example on their lives.

Mr Simeon was accustomed for a long course of years, to have every Friday what he called an open day, when all who chose went at six o'clock to take tea with him in his rooms, every one asking what questions he would, and receiving an answer longer or shorter as might be ... The numbers varied ... but not infrequently sixty or eighty were present, seated on chairs and benches arranged around the room ... Cordially, and with the suavity and politeness for which he was remarkable, he would welcome every student ... And if any stranger to him were introduced he would note down his name and college in his private pocketbook. After the arrivals had ceased, Mr Simeon's usual place was on an unbacked chair by the right hand of the fireplace ... His eye full of cheerful affection, his countenance slightly raised, so as not to seem fixed on any individual, he sought to please and encourage as well as instruct, and quickly placed every one as much as possible at ease ... In every possible way did Simeon endeavour to make those tea-parties both useful and agreeable, and to prevent disappointment to those young friends who had, as he loved to say, honoured him with their company.[4]

Many of those he met as students became lifelong and intimate friends. Here is John Babington:

Seventy-two years have passed this month since my first interview with Mr Simeon. I had just gone up [to university]. I had heard much of him as a most devoted servant of Christ; he was to my young mind a genuine hero ... and while my veneration for him was almost extreme, I rather shrank from very close contact with him. But all this vanished at the first interview. His kindness to me, a perfect stranger, his gentleness, the cordiality of my reception opened an entirely new view of his character and attached me to him with a union of admiration and affection that never passed away.[5]

Charles Simeon developed a particularly close and affectionate relationship with Henry Martyn, a brilliant mathematician and linguist, who was converted to Christ as a student through Simeon's ministry at Holy Trinity Church. Despite the closeness of their friendship, and the impact of Martyn's witness for Christ in Cambridge, Simeon encouraged and recommended him for missionary service in India. In July 1805, Henry Martyn sailed for India. In seven short years, he made an extraordinary impact in India and Persia through his Bible translations and fervent ministry, but his health was steadily declining due to chronic infections and as he was returning to England, he died, at the age of thirty-one.

In 1812, shortly before Martyn's death, a portrait had been commissioned and sent from Calcutta to London. Charles Simeon, who was present as the portrait was unpacked, wrote:

> I could not bear to look upon it but turned away, covering my face, and in spite of every effort to the contrary, crying aloud with anguish ... Shall I attempt to describe to you the veneration and the love with which I look at it ... In seeing how much he is worn, I am constrained to call to my relief the thought in whose service he has worn himself so much; and this reconciles me to the idea of weakness, of sickness, or even if God were so to appoint, of death itself . . . I behold in it all the mind of my beloved brother.[6]

The portrait was hung in Simeon's dining room, over the fireplace.

> He used often to look at it in his friends' presence, and to say, as he did so, with a peculiar loving emphasis, 'There see that blessed man! What an expression of countenance! No one looks at me as he does; he never takes his eyes off me, and seems always to be saying, "Be serious – be in earnest – don't trifle – don't trifle."' Then smiling at the picture and gently bowing he would add, 'And I won't trifle – I won't trifle.'[7]

Wherever he went, Charles Simeon devoted himself to establishing deep bonds with those who shared his vision for Christian service and witness. While travelling in Scotland in 1796 he met a minister called Alexander Stewart.

> In the evening Mr Stewart came up into my room; and we had much and useful conversation about the ministry. He complained of unprofitableness and was much affected during the conversation. We prayed together and parted very affectionately . . . He promised to write to me.[8]

Stewart wrote back on a number of occasions. Here is a letter some months after their meeting:

Ever since the few happy hours in which I was blessed with your company, I have daily thought with pleasure and gratitude of the Lord's loving kindness to me in sending his chosen servants so unexpectedly ... I wish I knew how to express my filial regard and attachment to one whom I have every reason to consider as my spiritual father. If Onesimus might call Paul his father, with like reason may I call Mr Simeon mine. For indeed I found from your conversation, your prayers, preaching and particularly from our short interview in your bedroom, more of religious impression and more of spiritual life and ardour infused into my soul than ever I was conscious of before.[9]

Simeon replied at once to his 'very, very dear friend':

There is an unaccountable union of heat with, or if I may so express myself, an outgoing of the soul toward some persons, which we feel instantaneously and we know not why. Such I felt almost the first instance I saw you my dear friend ... I hope it is an earnest of that everlasting union which our souls shall enjoy in the regions of life and love.[10]

Charles Simeon was part of a rich network of extraordinarily close and devoted evangelical Christian friends which stretched over Britain and across the world. The founding father of the network was perhaps Henry Venn, Rector of the parish of Yelling in Huntingdonshire. Venn soon struck up a close friendship with Simeon who travelled frequently from Cambridge to visit him. Venn wrote in 1782:

He has been over to see me six times in the last three months: he is calculated for great usefulness and is full of faith and love. My soul is always the better for his visits. Oh to flame as he does with zeal, and yet be beautified with meekness![11]

Eight years later, Venn was to write, 'On Monday my affectionate friend Simeon walked over and slept here. Oh how refreshing were his prayers! How profitable his conversation! We were all revived: he left a blessing behind him.'[12]

John Newton

The story of the slave trader who discovered the grace and forgiveness of God has been captured in many biographies and films. From his early ministry in the parish of Olney, to his later role as Rector of St Mary Woolnoth in the heart of London, Newton became one of the most influential voices in England in support of the evangelical faith. His hymns, including 'Amazing Grace', are still sung around the world. But the importance of friendship in his ministry is less well-remembered. His warmth, generosity, encouragement and faithfulness as a friend were celebrated at the time. As one contemporary wrote 'Mr. Newton could live no longer than he could love.'[13]

As I write these words, I have John Newton's four-volume collection of personal letters on my bookshelf, running to more than 2,000 pages.[14] And virtually every letter reflects his warmth, love, compassion, gentleness and godly concern for those he was writing to. As Ed Veale put it:

> Newton's prayerful, Scripture-saturated wisdom, and gentle affability, seen in countless loyal, honest, loving, Christ-centred friendships, which were carried out both in person and in letter, had a profound influence on countless evangelicals, and through them, on church and society for decades to come.[15]

Just one example of Newton's extraordinary faithfulness and love as a friend can be seen in his relationship with the poet William Cowper. Cowper had a history of deep depression and suicide attempts and had spent months in a sanatorium for the insane. It was in that period that he had been converted to Christ and shortly afterwards he met John Newton. The two men were drawn to each other at once and Newton arranged for Cowper to come to live in the parish of Olney. Sadly, Cowper's severe depression and suicidal preoccupations returned. Newton was often with him for several hours a day and, in April 1773, Cowper moved into the Vicarage for more than a year. Cowper had long spells of doubt, despair and spiritual darkness, but Newton remained a faithful and encouraging friend. Newton later wrote:

> For nearly twelve years we were seldom separated from seven hours at a time, when we were awake, and at home; the first six I passed daily admiring and aiming to imitate him; during the second six, I walked pensively with him in the valley of the shadow of death.[16]

William Cowper always recognised the extraordinary importance of Newton's faithful care:

> I found comforts in your visit, which have formerly sweetened all our interview. I knew you; knew you for the same shepherd who was sent to lead me out of the wilderness into the pasture where the Chief Shepherd feeds his flock, and felt my sentiments of affectionate friendship for you the same as ever.[17]

Building on their decades-long friendship, Newton and Cowper co-authored a collection of over three hundred songs, *The Olney Hymns*, first published in 1779. Newton's Preface to the hymnbook is a testimony to Cowper, 'It was intended as a monument to perpetuate the remembrance of an intimate and endeared friendship.'[18]

Newton founded an informal group of evangelical friends and pastors, the Eclectics Society, which included Charles Simeon and John Venn. He was not possessive or exclusive in his friendships, but rather a 'master networker, creating space for his friends to become friends with one another' – always, it seems, with an eye to the creative potential of these friendships for the kingdom.[19]

William Wilberforce

Hannah Wilberforce used to take her young nephew William to listen to John Newton's sermons. William, a boy of ten, used to listen enthralled to Newton, 'even reverencing him as a parent.'[20]

His mother became alarmed that Newton's influence on the young boy was 'turning him Methodist' and took him back to the North of England. Wilberforce became MP for Hull in 1784 and rapidly became a rising Parliamentary star. But in 1785 he was facing a spiritual crisis and was in deep distress. He was increasingly convicted of his need to commit his life to Christ's service but he knew that this would threaten both his popularity and his political career. He had to choose between Christ and the world, but he wanted both.

By late November, he had decided that if he was going to live for God he must withdraw from the world and become a pastor. In anguish, he turned to his boyhood hero, John Newton, now sixty years old and Rector of St Mary Woolnoth in the City of London. The fashionable world looked on Newton with contempt and suspicion and Wilberforce was painfully aware of the risk to his own reputation. He wrote a confidential letter to Newton:

> I wish to have some serious conversation with you . . . I have had ten thousand doubts within myself, whether or not I should discover myself to you; but every argument against it has its foundation in pride. I am sure you will hold yourself bound to let no one living know of this application, or of my visit, till I release you from the obligation . . . PS Remember that I must be secret, and that the gallery of the House is now so universally attended, that the face of a Member of Parliament is pretty well known.[21]

Wilberforce undertook a secret visit to Newton, walking twice round the square in Hoxton before he could persuade himself to knock at the door of Newton's home. Newton was overjoyed to hear the news of Wilberforce's spiritual quest and told him that he had been praying for him daily for the last sixteen years, since he had met him as a child.

So began a deep and unlikely friendship that was to have extraordinary consequences across the world. Newton became a wise, inspiring and supportive figure in Wilberforce's life, encouraging and emboldening him to continue in his political position, not for self-aggrandisement, but out of loyalty to Christ. Newton wrote to Wilberforce, 'It is hoped and believed that the Lord has raised you up for the good of His church and for the good of the nation.'[22]

With Newton's encouragement, Wilberforce developed a network of friends and political sympathisers, who became sneeringly known as 'The Saints'.[23] There was clearly a deep emotional resonance for Newton in Wilberforce's growing concern about the Atlantic slave trade. Newton often spoke to him remorsefully of his own time in 'the Trade' and of the African coast where he had once been 'a servant of slaves'.[24] Wilberforce's campaign against the slave trade met with years of hostility and frequent setbacks. It was Newton who stood by his side, spurring him on to persevere in his efforts in Parliament, reminding him that that his 'character may have a powerful though unobserved effect on others.'[25]

As the network of friends grew in size and influence, the wealthy evangelical benefactor Henry Thornton suggested to Wilberforce in 1792 that they set up a 'chummery' (!) at Battersea Rise, a small estate that Thornton had purchased in Clapham.[26] Several adjacent houses were purchased and Henry Venn's son, John Venn, was persuaded to join them as the vicar of Holy Trinity Clapham, the church which became their spiritual centre. As one writer put it, 'they were powerfully bound together by shared moral and spiritual values, by religious mission and social activism, by love for each other and by marriage.'[27] They were people for whom friendship was of the utmost importance. 'They lived in each other's spare rooms, married each other's brothers and sisters, prayed together, worked together, dreamed and schemed together, consoled each other and criticised each other with ruthless honesty.'[28]

I am reminded of the famous quote by the Church Father Tertullian, describing the lives of the early Christians. 'One in mind and soul, we do not hesitate to share our earthly goods with one another. All things are common among us but our wives.'[29]

This is not the place to tell the story about the subsequent impact this group of friends had on England and across the world – the abolition of the slave trade, the creation of the Church Missionary Society and the Bible Society, the revival of evangelical Christianity and biblical preaching in the Church of England, the transformation of the British Parliament and so on and on. My reason for including this chapter is to point to the deep, intimate and committed friendships which were at the heart of this remarkable story from evangelical history. Without those friendships, the impact of the lives of Wilberforce and the others would have been very different.

In his mid-seventies, John Newton wrote to his friend, John Ryland:

Many kind and dear friends the Lord has provided to comfort and counsel me in my pilgrimage. My friends have dropped off in succession, like leaves from a tree in autumn. But I hope to meet them again. Oh! What a meeting that will be, where we shall all, without a cloud or veil, see Him in whose presence is fullness of joy.[30]

10
Transforming friendship

The title of this book has a deliberate double meaning. On the one hand, I have tried to provide my personal tribute to the transformative power of gospel-crafted friendship, and to the way in which my closest friendships have transformed my life and continue to do so.

But the title is also a reference to the fact that here in the early years of the twenty-first century, we need to *reimagine* friendship. We have seen how the very word 'friendship' in English has become trivialised, distorted and corrupted by many forces: the sexualisation of the culture, the ubiquity of social media and the commercialisation of internet 'friendship', the appalling abuse scandals involving prominent Christian leaders, the hermeneutic of suspicion and the fear of being accused of inappropriate behaviour.

We cannot go back to the previous age and culture in which John Stott and his contemporaries lived. We cannot ignore what we have learnt from the tragic cases of sexual, emotional and spiritual abuse which have belatedly come to prominence. Instead, we need to reflect and build on the rapid growth in understanding that has occurred. Now we understand much more about how friendship can go wrong, about the risks of emotional and psychological coercion and control within the context of Christian relationships and particularly in intergenerational friendships.

I return to the helpful analogy that Jim Packer provided. Living in a wise and godly way is like trying to drive with skill and care down a narrow and twisty road. It's a process of continual improvisation in the perpetually changing contingencies and choices which daily life presents. In order to drive safely, we need to know, understand and follow the rules and boundaries, which are there to keep us from disaster. We need to be ruthlessly clear-sighted and realistic about the risks. We are free to innovate, to improvise, to live creatively and to the glory of God, provided that we respect the rules and boundaries of safe friendships. It is realism and wisdom that bring freedom: freedom to navigate the path together with safety, security and joy.

How can we foster a culture in which healthy, deep and intimate, gospel-crafted friendships can flourish?

It seems to me as though we are only just starting on the journey of reimagining Christian friendship, in the new relational landscape in which we find ourselves. I don't feel qualified to lay down any specific guidelines or recommendations to the church as a whole. All I can do is hesitantly offer some preliminary suggestions to readers of this book.

First, it's clear that we need to lay a foundation of both biblical and practical teaching about healthy gospel-crafted friendships. There is a wealth of biblical material to be explored and mined, and yet the topic of friendship seems to have been under-emphasised, if not ignored.

Second, we need to avoid an unhealthy overemphasis on sexual and romantic relationships and find ways of highlighting the fundamental importance of healthy non-sexual friendships to Christian living and spiritual formation. We need to encourage each follower of Christ to form and nurture a rich network of healthy friendships, including intergenerational Paul–Timothy relationships. I have heard it said that 'every Christian needs a Timothy, a Barnabas (an encourager) and a Paul.'

Third, we need to celebrate and learn from the many examples of healthy, gospel-crafted friendships that already exist in our own communities. At the same time, we need to learn from the friendship examples of Christians who have gone before, including the rich friendship culture of previous generations of evangelical Christians.

Fourth, we need to ensure that everyone is aware of, and agrees to, the essential boundaries that healthy, gospel-crafted friendships depend upon. We also need to be aware of the red flags that indicate that a relationship has become unhealthy and dangerous, and ensure that everyone in our communities understands how to raise safeguarding concerns about friendships that are becoming unhealthy.

Finally, we need to be encouraging self-reflection, transparency and some form of regular peer review and accountability for all older individuals pursuing intergenerational friendships.

But how do I start?

Many people in our culture, and perhaps especially men, feel that, although they may have many superficial acquaintances, they do not have any close friends, people with whom they can be completely honest and share their hearts. Many start their adult lives with a group of friends from college or their workplace but, as time goes by, they lose touch and their friendships diminish and dwindle. So, what practical steps can we take to create healthy and deep friendships?

The first thing to recognise is that *healthy, gospel-crafted friendships don't happen accidentally.* They need to be intentionally nurtured, fed and developed. And this takes time and purposeful action. As Rico Tice put it to me, 'Love is a four letter word spelt T-I-M-E.' Part of the problem of our modern age seems to be that we have so many other distractions and demands on our time that we have no spare capacity for building and investing in friendships. It's all a question of priorities. Is nurturing a friendship more important than catching up on the latest film release? If we are going to develop deep, intimate and healthy friendships then it is obvious that we need to see this as a high priority and put friendship before other interests and ways of spending time.

Second, *examine your motives.* Whereas we have unbreakable obligations to our biological family members and relatives, and we have duties and responsibilities to our Christian brothers and sisters, our friendships are *freely chosen.* We are free, prayerfully, to reach out to those with whom we feel an affinity, a connection, a spiritual intuition, a personal chemistry.

But of course, we need to reflect on our motives. Why do I want to reach out to this particular person? Is it because I have a need that they can meet? Is there an ulterior motive, a desire to use the other person for my own agenda? Or do I genuinely wish to reach out to the other person out of love and respect for their own interests and well-being? Do I wish ultimately to create a friendship that is crafted out of the heart of the gospel, a relationship that reflects the truth, honesty, humility, joy and sacrifice of the gospel?

Third, *take the initiative.* We saw how much time John Stott spent in reaching out to his friends, writing letters, making phone calls, sending cards. Mark Labberton told me how he had learnt from John Stott the same practice of continually reaching out to others. 'I just wanted to check in with you', 'What are the challenges you are facing at the moment? How can I pray for you?' As Mark told me, the delight of the encounter is that there was no underlying programme or strategy. It was the unexpected delight of establishing communion with another. And in reaching out to the other, I am of course opening myself to the possibility of rejection and hurt. All genuine friendship involves an element of vulnerability and openness to hurt.

Fourth, *find common interests.* As C. S. Lewis said all friendships are 'about something'. They are not aimless and directionless. There are shared enthusiasms, interests and goals. And although gospel-crafted friendships are ultimately orientated towards the good of the other person and to spiritual growth in Christlikeness, they are also based on shared human interests.

Fifth, *ask good questions.* Respect and care for the other involves asking questions and listening carefully and remembering the answers. The questions that Mark Labberton mentioned are a good starting point, 'What's going on in your life at the moment? What challenges and issues are you facing? What are you most stressed and anxious about? How can I pray for you?'

Sixth, when it seems safe and appropriate, be prepared to *share some of your own vulnerabilities.* As we humble ourselves before the other person and share some of our own hurts and vulnerabilities, we are modelling the servant-heartedness and humility which is at the heart of gospel-crafted friendships. And when there has been hurt, failure and misunderstanding between us we need to ask for forgiveness and grace. As I have researched and written this book, I have been painfully reminded of my own inadequacies and failures as a loyal and committed covenant-friend. But I am grateful for the forgiveness, understanding and kindness that I continue to receive from others. As Peter put it, 'Above all, keep loving one another earnestly, since love covers a multitude of sins' (1 Peter 4:8).

Seventh, *pray for your friends*. As we saw earlier, the wonderful international network of relationships that John Stott established, and his remarkable memory for names and details of individual lives, was rooted in his daily practice of faithful, disciplined prayer for his friends around the world.

Finally, *keep going*. Nurturing meaningful and healthy friendships requires time and persistence. As Bishop J. C. Ryle noted: 'Friendship halves our troubles and doubles our joys.'[1]

Gospel-shaped friendships both *model* and *mediate* God's love for us. We learn the meaning of God's *chesed* by experiencing the covenant love of a dear and loyal friend who sticks with us through thick and thin. We understand God's faithfulness by tasting a human 'love that will not let me go'. But in those same friendships, God himself is loving us through the love of our friends. The medieval author Bernard of Clairvaux said 'Christ himself kisses us in the love of our friends.' Speaking personally, this has been a precious reality for me at times when I have been in deep darkness and despair. The kindness, gentleness and encouragement of my friends, and my wife Celia, have embodied the very tangible presence of Christ.

The God who proclaims, 'I have loved you with an everlasting love; I have drawn you with unfailing kindness [*chesed*]' (Jeremiah 31:3 NIV), is drawing us to himself through the love of our friends.

It's a valuable exercise to reflect back on all the closest friendships we have experienced, starting with our earliest memories and gradually coming forward to the present. Who were the individuals that God has used to reach out to you? What was it that you saw in each of their lives or experienced in their friendship? What did each one show you about the character and the heart of God himself? Spend time in thanking God for his everlasting covenant love and for the friends in your life whom he has used to draw you closer to himself.

How could it be that our friends have been so significant in our spiritual journeys? As C. S. Lewis puts it:

A secret master of ceremonies has been at work. Christ, who said to the disciples, 'You have not chosen me, but I have chosen you,' can truly say to every group of Christian friends, 'You have not chosen one another but I have chosen you for one another.'[2]

The God, who in his very triune being is both union and communion, has created us for communion with one another and with himself. Human friendship is part of the blessings of creation and for millennia, people of all communities and backgrounds have built deep and faithful bonds. But through Christ, human communion has become gospel-shaped and friendship become an embodied enactment and mysterious anticipation of the ultimate communion that is to come.

Human love comes in many wonderful forms and each one provides a unique picture of our relationship with God and a taste of the world that is to come. There is familial love, the love of a parent for a child. There is self-sacrificial love, *agape* love that pours itself out for the good of the other. There is erotic romantic love that enables those with the gift of marriage to become one flesh with another human being, which Paul says is ultimately intended as a human representation of the love between Christ and the Church (Ephesians 5:32). And there is friendship, gospel-crafted, face-to-face, joyful covenant love. And in each of these wonderful, unique and endlessly fascinating forms of human love, Christ himself is saying – 'Here I am.'

C. S. Lewis, in his book *The Four Loves*, paints one of the most evocative pictures of friendship I have come across:

Those are the golden sessions . . . when our slippers are on, our feet spread out before the blaze and our drinks at our elbows;

when the whole world, and something beyond the world, opens itself to our minds as we talk . . . and an Affection mellowed by the years enfolds us. Life – natural life – has no better gift to give. Who could have deserved it?[3]

As I have reflected on the deepest friendships of my life, it is those special moments which stand out. That sense of joy in companionship, the peace which is a balm to anxiety and stress, the shared understanding which doesn't need to be put into words, the humour which is meaningless to outsiders. And it has struck me that these special moments of friendship reflect the biblical concept of Sabbath.

Yes, we all have duties, vocations and responsibilities to others which need to be fulfilled. These are the preoccupations of the six days of work in which we spend most of our waking hours. But every so often we are given the gift of wonderful shared moments of friendship which belong to the Sabbath. They point back to the moment in Eden when God chose to walk in the garden with his friends. And they are a precious foretaste of the age to come.

As Drew Hunter put it, 'Think about your most joyful moments with friends. Now take that joy, multiply it by ten thousand and project it into the eternal future . . . History ends . . . with the laughter of friends.'[4]

It is only in our 'hours-off,' only in our moments of permitted festivity, that we find an analogy. Dance and game are frivolous, unimportant down here; for 'down here' is not their natural place. Here, they are a moment's rest from the life we were placed here to live.

But in this world everything is upside down. That which, if it could be prolonged here, would be a truancy, is likest that which in a better country is the End of ends. Joy is the serious business of Heaven.[5]

(C. S. Lewis)

Notes

1 A brief history of friendship

1 The lyrics can be found from many internet sources including on Hymnary: https://hymnary.org/text/my_song_is_love_ unknown.

2 I have been unable to find the source for this quotation.

3 My material on friendship in the classical world has been derived from a number of sources but especially Liz Carmichael, *Friendship: Interpreting Christian Love* (London and New York: T&T Clark International, 2004), pp. 7–35.

4 Quoted in Carmichael, *Friendship*, p. 17.

5 Aristotle, *Nicomachean Ethics*, Books 8 and 9 (350 BC). See also Carmichael, *Friendship*, pp. 15–22.

6 Cicero, *De Amicitia* (44 BC). See also Carmichael, *Friendship*, pp. 25–32.

7 Cicero, *De Amicitia*, quoted in Carmichael, *Friendship*, p. 31.

8 In what follows I have used material in particular from Charles Taylor, *Sources of the Self: The Making of the Modern Identity* (Cambridge, MA: Harvard University Press, 1989); Charles Taylor, *A Secular Age* (Cambridge, MA: Harvard University Press, 2007); and Carl Trueman, *The Rise and Triumph of the Modern Self: Cultural Amnesia, Expressive Individualism, and the Road to the Sexual Revolution* (Wheaton, IL: Crossway, 2020).

9 René Descartes, *The Philosophical Writings of Descartes* (trans. J. Cottingham, R. Stoothoff and D. Murdoch) (Cambridge and New York: Cambridge University Press, 1985): doi:10.1017/ CBO9780511805042.

10 John Stuart Mill, *On Liberty* (1859).

11 Jean-Jacques Rousseau, *The Social Contract* (1762).

12 Jean-Jacques Rousseau, *Discourses* (1750), p. 8.

13 Quoted in Trueman, *The Rise and Triumph of the Modern Self*, pp. 151–3.

14 Quoted in Trueman, *The Rise and Triumph of the Modern Self*, p. 153.

2 The sexualisation of friendship and the 'hermeneutic of suspicion'

1 See Florence Rush, *The Best Kept Secret: Sexual Abuse of Children* (New York: McGraw-Hill, 1980) and Jeffrey Masson, *The Assault on Truth: Freud's Suppression of the Seduction Theory* (New York: Farrar, Straus and Giroux, 1984).

2 You can still see Freud's original chaise longue, described as one of the most significant pieces of domestic furniture in Western civilisation, in the Freud Museum in North London.

3 Roger Scruton, quotation source unknown.

4 Friedrich Nietzsche, *Twilight of the Idols* (1889), chapter 6.

5 For an accessible introduction, see Gary Gutting, *Foucault: A Very Short Introduction* (Oxford: Oxford University Press, 2019).

6 Desmond Morris, *The Naked Ape: A Zoologist's Study of the Human Animal*, 1st edn (London: Jonathan Cape, 1967).

7 P. V. Liao and J. Dollin, 'Half a Century of the Oral Contraceptive Pill: Historical review and view to the future', *Canadian Family Physician* (2012) 58: e757–60.

8 Robin Dunbar et al, 'The Naked Ape at 50', *The Observer*, 24 September 2017.

9 Malcolm Muggeridge, *Muggeridge through the Microphone: BBC Radio and Television*, ed. Christopher Ralling, with drawings by Trog (London: Fontana, 1969).

10 Paul Ricoeur, *De l'interprétation. Essai sur Freud (L'ordre philosophique)* (Paris: Éditions du Seuil, 1965).

11 Rita Felski, 'Critique and the Hermeneutics of Suspicion', *M/C Journal* (2011) 15(1): https://doi.org/10.5204/mcj.431.

12 Christopher Watkin, *Biblical Critical Theory: How the Bible's Unfolding Story Makes Sense of Modern Life and Culture* (Grand Rapids, MI: Zondervan, 2023), p. 122.

3 Friendship in the Bible

1 There are a few books, however, which I have found very helpful, especially Saul Olyan, *Friendship in the Hebrew Bible* (New Haven, CT: Yale University Press, 2017), and Carmichael, *Friendship*, which I have already mentioned.

2 Olyan, *Friendship in the Hebrew Bible*, p. 16.

3 The *ch* in *chesed* is soft, pronounced as in lo*ch*.

4 The words are Chris Wright's, personal communication.

5 I'm very grateful to Chris Wright for his valuable insights on this passage.

6 Thanks again to Chris Wright for his insights on the passage.

7 Gary Inrig, *Quality Friendship* (Chicago, IL: Moody Press, 1981).

8 Fyodor Dostoevsky, *The Grand Inquisitor* (1880).

9 The insight is Chris Wright's.

10 C. S. Lewis, *The Four Loves* (London: Collins, 2010, ebook edition).

11 Tim Keller, sermon on Spiritual Friendship, 2008.

12 Mark Labberton, private conversation.

13 Chris Wright, private conversation.

14 Pirkei Avot 4:13, *The Mishnah*: https://www.sefaria.org/Pirkei_Avot.4.13

15 Richard Bauckham, 'The Future of Jesus Christ', *Scottish Evangelical Bulletin of Theology* (1998), pp. 97–110.

16 I am aware that some have suggested that the Beloved Disciple was not the same person as John the son of Zebedee. See for example Richard Bauckham, *Jesus and the Eyewitnesses: The Gospels as Eyewitness Testimony*, 2nd edn (Grand Rapids, MI: Eerdmans, 2017). However, in this study I have adopted the traditional view that the Beloved Disciple was the son of Zebedee.

17 Andrew Cornes, personal communication.

18 See Gafcon (29 July 2020): https://www.gafcon.org/devotion/lazarus-martha-and-mary-friends-of-jesus

19 See D. A. Carson, *The Gospel According to John*. Pillar New Testament Commentary (Leicester: IVP, 1991).

20 Carmen Caltagirone, *Friendship as Sacrament* (New York: Alba House, 1988), p. 38.

Notes

21 Spurgeon's Sermons, No 1552, 1880, vol 26: https://ccel.org/ccel/
spurgeon/sermons26/sermons26.xli.html

22 John Stott, *The Message of Romans: God's Good News for the World*
(Leicester: IVP, 1994), p. 394.

4 Gospel-crafted friendships

1 Lewis, *The Four Loves*, p. 48.

2 Henri Nouwen, *Out of Solitude: Three Meditations on the Christian
Life* (Notre Dame, IN: Ave Maria Press, 2004), p. 18.

3 Caltagirone, *Friendship as Sacrament*, p. 23.

4 Henri Nouwen, *Adam: God's Beloved*, Kindle edn (New York:
Orbis Books, 2022), p. 50.

5 Paul Woolley, 'John Stott: What every Christian should know about
this unlikely radical', *Premier Christianity* magazine (February
2021).

6 J. I. Packer, *Knowing God*, 3rd edn (London: Hodder & Stoughton
2005), pp. 115–16.

7 Henri Nouwen, *The Road to Daybreak: A Spiritual Journey* (London:
Darton, Longman & Todd, 2013), p. 65.

8 It's not possible to find a biblical proof text that our closest friendships
will persist into the new heaven and new earth, but I think there are
strong hints within the New Testament that this will be the case. The
resurrected Jesus enjoys eating food together with his human friends
and promises them that he will feast with them in the age to come
(Matthew 26:29). Paul encourages the Christians in Thessalonica not
to grieve without hope for those of their number who have fallen
asleep, because they will be reunited at the resurrection and will
always be together 'with the Lord' (1 Thessalonians 4:13–17).

9 Henri Nouwen, *The Inner Voice of Love* (New York: Doubleday,
1996).

10 Dietrich Bonhoeffer, *Life Together*, Geffrey B. Kelly (ed), trans.
James H. Burtness (Minneapolis: MN: Fortress Press, 2015), p. 9.

5 Would you like to have a cup of coffee with me?

1 John Stott in John Eddison (ed), *Bash: A Study in Spiritual Power*
(London: Marshall, Morgan & Scott, 1983), p. 58.

2 Eddison, *Bash*, p. 59.

3 Eddison, *Bash*, p. 59.

4 Timothy Dudley-Smith, *John Stott: The Making of a Leader* (Downers Grove, IL: InterVarsity Press, 1999), p. 143.

5 Dudley-Smith, *John Stott: The Making of a Leader*, p. 238.

6 See, for example, Dudley-Smith, *John Stott: The Making of a Leader*; Timothy Dudley-Smith, *John Stott: A Global Ministry* (IVP, 2001); Roger Steer, *Inside Story: The Life of John Stott* (Downer's Grove, IL: IVP, 2009); Alister Chapman, *Godly Ambition: John Stott and the Evangelical Movement* (Oxford and New York: Oxford University Press, 2012).

7 Taken from a transcript of John Stott's talk at the inaugural meeting of the London Institute for Contemporary Christianity, 1982, kindly provided by Brian Ladd.

8 The following section includes some material adapted from my article, 'John Stott and Political Theology', *The Big Picture Online Magazine*, Kirby Laing Centre (August 2021): https://kirbylaingcentre.co.uk/the-big-picture/online-magazine/issue-02/john-stott-and-political-theology/

9 Vinoth Ramachandra, 'True Leadership' (28 February 2021): https://vinothramachandra.wordpress.com/2021/02/28/true-leadership/

10 John Stott, *I Believe in Preaching* (London: Hodder & Stoughton, 1982), pp. 195–7.

11 C. S. Lewis, 'The Inner Ring', in *The Weight of Glory: A Collection of Lewis' Most Moving Addresses* (London: Collins, 2013), p. 146.

12 Stott in Eddison, *Bash*, p. 59.

13 John Stott, *The Contemporary Christian: Applying God's Word to Today's World* (Downer's Grove, IL: IVP, 1992), p. 358.

14 Stott, *The Contemporary Christian*, p. 111.

15 John Stott and Christopher J. H. Wright, *Christian Mission in the Modern World* (Downer's Grove, IL: IVP, 2015), p. 110.

16 Some of this material is adapted from the chapter I contributed to the book, Chris Wright (ed), *John Stott: A Portrait by His Friends* (IVP, 2011).

17 John Stott, *The Radical Disciple: Some Neglected Aspects of Our Calling* (Downers Grove, IL 2010), p. 112.

6 John Stott and his friends from across the world

1 John Stott, *Guard the Gospel* (IVP, 1973), pp. 120–1.
2 John Stott, 'When I Feel Most Alive', London Institute of Contemporary Christianity, https://www.youtube.com/watch?v=MDPqw-LAuaU.0
3 David Zac Niringiye, 'The Gospel and the Public Square', in Laura S. Meitzner Yoder (ed), *Living Radical Discipleship: Inspired by John Stott* (Langham Global Library, 2021), pp. 47–8.
4 I'm very grateful to Pilar Cruz, Eidi and Saúl Jr and Matthew Smith who provided this information and gave permission for me to publish it.
5 The quotations from Ruth Padilla DeBorst are taken from *The Stott Legacy* podcast episode 8: https://thestottlegacy.podbean.com/e/ruth-padilla-deborst/ and from the recording of Ruth's contribution to John Stott's memorial service in St Paul's Cathedral, 13 January 2021: https://www.youtube.com/watch?v=FxpxxTEvgMk
6 Ramachandra, 'True Leadership'.
7 http://www.mahalirarantrust.com
8 I'm very grateful to Mercy Abraham Imondi for permission to use her words, and to Mary Currie who played a key role in making them available.
9 Mark Labberton, private conversation.
10 Matthew Smith, private conversation.
11 Rico Tice, 'Reflections on the Christlike Leadership of John Stott', Good Book Company (25 March 2021): https://www.thegoodbook.co.uk/blog/encouraging-articles/2021/03/25/reflections-on-the-christlike-leadership-of-john-s/
12 Wright, *John Stott: A Portrait by His Friends*.
13 Timothy Dudley-Smith in Wright, *John Stott: A Portrait*, p. 43.
14 Myra Chave Jones in Wright, *John Stott: A Portrait*, p. 38.
15 Frances Whitehead in Wright, *John Stott: A Portrait*, p. 59.
16 Ajith Fernando in Wright, *John Stot: A Portrait*, p. 109.
17 Chris Wright in Wright, *John Stott: A Portrait*, p. 149.
18 Peter Harris in Wright, *John Stott: A Portrait*, p. 161.

7 Paul–Timothy friendships

1 I am, of course, aware that many critical scholars have questioned the authenticity of the Pastoral Epistles, regarding them as 'pious forgeries'. John Stott addresses this issue with characteristic rigour in his volume *The Message of 1 Timothy and Titus* (IVP, 1996) and it seems appropriate to summarise his conclusions. 'The internal evidence in favour of Pauline authorship is strong. Paul includes many personal references both to himself and to his relationship with Timothy . . . If all these human details, emotions and concerns were in fact invented years later by a pseudonymous Christian writer, this would seem both extraordinarily creative and also manipulative.' (p. 83). The genuineness of the Pastoral Epistles was almost universally accepted by the church from the beginning, with the first probable allusions to them dating from AD 95. The external witness to the authenticity of the three Pastoral Letters continued as an unbroken tradition until Friedrich Schleiermacher rejected the authenticity of 1 Timothy in 1807. Stott concludes, 'The case for the Pauline authorship of the Pastorals still stands. Both the internal claims and the external witness are strong, substantial and stubborn. The burden of proof rests on those who deny them.'(p. 83).

2 Stott, *The Message of 1 Timothy and Titus*, p. 6.

3 Stott, *The Message of 1 Timothy and Titus*, p. 40.

4 Tice, 'Reflections on the Christlike Leadership of John Stott'.

5 James K. A. Smith, *How to Inhabit Time: Understanding the Past, Facing the Future, Living Faithfully Now* (Grand Rapids, MI: Brazos Press, 2022), p. 135.

6 Stott, *Guard the Gospel*, p. 29.

7 Mark Meynell, *And Who Is My Neighbour? The Imago Dei and the Exercise of Power*, Primer 11 (Oak Hill College, 2021): https://www.academia.edu/83872795/And_Who_is_My_Neighbour_The_Imago_Dei_and_the_Exercise_of_Power_

8 Henri Nouwen, *In the Name of Jesus: Reflections on Christian Leadership* (London: Darton, Longman & Todd, 1989).

9 Erik Johnson, 'How to Be an Effective Mentor', *Christianity Today* (2000): https://www.christianitytoday.com/pastors/2000/spring/how-to-be-an-effective-mentor.html

10 See, for example, https://mentoringgroup.com/what-is-coaching.html

11 Cheri Rowe, 'A New Way to Care? Changing models of pastoral care', *Thirtyone:eight magazine* (10 November 2021): https://thirtyoneeight.org/together-magazine/a-new-way-to-care-changing-models-of-pastoral-care/

12 Attributed to various people, including R. J. Sproul, D. Thambyrajah Niles, D. L. Moody and Charles Spurgeon.

8 How friendships go wrong

1 Lisa Oakley and Justin Humphreys, *Escaping the Maze of Spiritual Abuse: Creating Healthy Christian Cultures* (London: SPCK, 2019), p. 22.

2 Albert D. Biderman, 'Communist Attempts to Elicit False Confessions from Air Force Prisoners of War', *Bulletin of the New York Academy of Medicine* (1957) 33, pp. 616–25.

3 Mark Stibbe, Foreword, in Oakley and Humphreys, *Escaping the Maze of Spiritual Abuse*.

4 Oakley and Humphreys, *Escaping the Maze of Spiritual Abuse*, p. 64.

5 Marcus Honeysett, *Powerful Leaders? When Church Leadership Goes Wrong and How to Prevent It* (IVP, 2022), is a valuable and insightful resource in this regard.

9 Simeon, Newton and Wilberforce

1 John Stott, Introduction, in James Houston (ed), *Evangelical Preaching: An Anthology of Sermons by Charles Simeon* (Vancouver: Regent College Publishing, 2003), p. xxvii.

2 Stott in Houston, *Evangelical Preaching*, p. xxvii.

3 Stott in Houston, *Evangelical Preaching*, p. xxxviii.

4 Handley Moule, *Charles Simeon* (Methuen, 1892), Kindle edn, 2715.

5 Moule, *Charles Simeon*, 2223.

6 Moule, *Charles Simeon*, 1755.

7 Moule, *Charles Simeon*, 1755.

8 Moule, *Charles Simeon*, 2011.

9 Moule, *Charles Simeon*, 2044.

10 Moule, *Charles Simeon*, 2055.

11 Moule, *Charles Simeon*, 352.

12 Moule, *Charles Simeon*, 480.

13 Richard Cecil, *Memoirs of the Rev. John Newton*, 1808: https://gracegems.org/Newton/Memoirs.htm.

14 *The Works of John Newton* (Edinburgh: Banner of Truth Trust, 2015).

15 Ed Veale, 'John Newton and the Gift of Friendship in Reformed Spiritual Formation', unpublished essay (Oak Hill College, 2020).

16 Josiah Bull, *Life of John Newton* (Edinburgh: Banner of Truth Trust, 2007), p. 135.

17 Quoted in John Piper, 'Depression Fought Hard to Have Him: William Cowper (1731–1800)', 2019: https://www.desiringgod.org/articles/depression-fought-hard-to-have-him.

18 John Newton, Preface, in John Newton and William Cowper, *The Olney Hymns* (1779): https://www.johnnewton.org/Groups/223001/The_John_Newton/new_menus/Hymns/Olney_Hymns_Preface/Olney_Hymns_Preface.aspx.

19 Veale, 'John Newton and the Gift of Friendship in Reformed Spiritual Formation'.

20 John Pollock, *Wilberforce* (Eastbourne: Kingsway Publications, 2007), p. 24.

21 Robert Isaac Wilberforce and Samuel Wilberforce, *The Life of William Wilberforce*, London (1843), p. 47, quoted in John Piper, 'Tribute to William Wilberforce' (2007): https://www.desiringgod.org/articles/tribute-to-william-wilberforce-1.

22 Quoted in Piper, 'Tribute to William Wilberforce'.

23 Pollock, *Wilberforce*, p. 97.

24 Pollock, *Wilberforce*, p. 78.

25 John Newton's letter to William Wilberforce, 21 July 1796: https://www.christian.org.uk/news/on-this-day-newton-urged-wilberforce-to-keep-going.

26 Pollock, *Wilberforce*, p. 157.

27 Stephen Tomkins, *The Clapham Sect: How Wilberforce's Circle Transformed Britain* (Oxford: Lion Hudson, 2010), p. 11.

28 Tomkins, *The Clapham Sect*, p. 12.

29 Tertullian, *Apology* (AD 197): http://www.logoslibrary.org/tertullian/apology/39.html.

30 John Newton, *Wise Counsel: John Newton's Letters to John Ryland, Jr* (Edinburgh: Banner of Truth Trust, 2009), p. 314.

10 Transforming friendship

1 J. C. Ryle, *The Best Friend* (1878): https://gracegems.org/Ryle/best_friend.htm.
2 Lewis, *The Four Loves*, p. 64.
3 Lewis, *The Four Loves*, p. 52.
4 Drew Hunter, *Made for Friendship: The Relationship That Halves Our Sorrows and Doubles Our Joys* (Wheaton, IL: Crossway, 2018).
5 C. S. Lewis, *Letters to Malcolm: Chiefly on Prayer* (London: Geoffrey Bles, 1964), p. 122.

Further resources

Books on friendship

Drew Hunter, *Made for Friendship: The Relationship That Halves Our Sorrows and Doubles Our Joys* (Wheaton, IL: Crossway, 2018)

Liz Carmichael, *Friendship: Interpreting Christian Love* (London and New York: T&T Clark International, 2004)

Vaughan Roberts, *True Friendship: Walking Shoulder to Shoulder* (Leyland: 10Publishing, 2013)

Carmen Caltagirone, *Friendship as Sacrament* (New York: Alba House, 1988)

Saul Olyan, *Friendship in the Hebrew Bible* (New Haven, CT: Yale University Press, 2017)

Phil Knox, *The Best of Friends: Choose Wisely, Care Well* (IVP, 2023)

Books on 'spiritual abuse' and coercive control

Lisa Oakley and Justin Humphreys, *Escaping the Maze of Spiritual Abuse: Creating Healthy Christian Cultures* (London: SPCK, 2019)

Diane Langberg, *Suffering and the Heart of God: How Trauma Destroys and Christ Restores* (Greensboro, NC: New Growth Press, 2015)

Diane Langberg, *Redeeming Power: Understanding Authority and Abuse in the Church* (Grand Rapids, MI: Brazos Press, 2020)

Marcus Honeysett, *Powerful Leaders? When Church Leadership Goes Wrong* (IVP, 2022)